Praise for John W. Evans's
*Young Widower*

Winner of the 2014 Foreword Reviews
INDIEFAB Book of the Year Award

"In this honest depiction of his deceased wife and their loving but complicated marriage, and in his willingness to end his story without easy redemption, Evans avoids the predictable arc of many memoirs. . . . Thanks to honest and sadly beautiful books like *Young Widower*, we are at the very least helpless together. We can't go on, we'll go on."
—*Los Angeles Review of Books*

"A tragic story told with such grace and artistry that the complex exploration of grief is finally revealed as redemptive. The honesty of John Evans's writing is unfaltering and deeply impressive."
—Kevin Casey, author of *A State of Mind*

"While the haunting account of the day Katie died is especially riveting, it is the unfolding and cathartic grieving process that underpins and elevates this heartbreaking tale."
—*Booklist*

"For those times when life is bitter and unreasonable, there are stories like John's—books that accept the ugliness of both death and survival and remind us to be grateful and angry and preciously alive."
—*Books J'Adore*

"An urgent, palpably emotional account of coping with extreme grief."
—*Kirkus*

"Though the tragedy of Evans's title is borne out, his memoir brims with maturity and authenticity, and it should find a ready readership with those who have lived through incredible loss. *Young Widower* is both a loving tribute to a cherished spouse and a testament to survival."

—*ForeWord Reviews*

"This book brims with unforgettable images and moments, but Evans's greatest achievement is allowing readers to see his wife, Katie, as he did—not as a saint or as a martyr, but as a passionate and dynamic and flawed woman whom he deeply loved."

—Justin St. Germain, author of *Son of a Gun*

"A riveting and devastating chronicle of the tragedy that brutally ended a life and a marriage, and the aftermath of grief. Told with uncompromising candor and poetic precision, *Young Widower* is an unforgettable memoir of unrelenting beauty."

—Patricia Engel, author of *The Veins of the Ocean*

SHOULD I STILL WISH

AMERICAN LIVES

Series editor: Tobias Wolff

# Should I
# Still Wish

A MEMOIR

*John W. Evans*

UNIVERSITY OF NEBRASKA PRESS
*Lincoln and London*

Library of Congress Cataloging-in-Publication Data
Names: Evans, John W. (John William), 1977– author.
Title: Should I still wish: a memoir / John W. Evans.
Description: Lincoln: University of Nebraska
Press, [2017] | Series: American lives
Identifiers: LCCN 2016014263 (print)
LCCN 2016031248 (ebook)
ISBN 9780803295223 (paperback: alk. paper)
ISBN 9780803295797 (epub)
ISBN 9780803295803 (mobi)
ISBN 9780803295810 ( pdf)
Subjects: LCSH: Evans, John W. (John William),
1977– | Widowers—United States—Biography.
| Wives—Death—Psychological aspects. | Loss
(Psychology) | Adjustment (Psychology) | Man-woman
relationships. | Remarriage. | BISAC: BIOGRAPHY
& AUTOBIOGRAPHY / Personal Memoirs.
Classification: LCC HQ1058.5.U5 E927 2017 (print)
| LCC HQ1058.5.U5 (ebook) | DDC 155.2/4—dc23
LC record available at https://lccn.loc.gov/2016014263

Set in Garamond Premier by John Klopping.
Designed by N. Putens.

*for Walt, Sam, and Monty,*
*who might wonder,*

*and*

*for Cait,*
*always*

Thence issuing we again beheld the stars.

—*Inferno*, Canto XXXIV

Remember this, I remember telling myself, hang on to this. I could feel it all skittering away, whatever conjunction of beauty and improbability I had stumbled upon.

—Patricia Hampl, "Red Sky in the Morning"

# CONTENTS

# ACKNOWLEDGMENTS

My deepest thanks to my editor, Alicia Christensen, for recognizing this book and championing its place at the University of Nebraska Press. Thanks also to Rosemary Vestal, Tayler Lord, Maggie Boyles, and Martyn Beeny for helping this book to find its readers and to the design team for the beautiful cover. Thanks to Julie Kimmel for her careful editing eye. I am grateful to the Creative Writing Program at Stanford University for its generous support, especially Eavan Boland and Ken Fields. Thanks to Ray Peterson. Special thanks to Johnathan Johnson, Katharine Noel, Tricia O'Neill, Shannon Pufahl, Thayer Lindner, and Don Mayer for reading various early drafts, and to Cait, for reading all of them.

SHOULD I STILL WISH

# Leaving Indiana

I left Indiana and drove toward happiness. I meant to get far to one side of the map. In two or three weeks, I told myself, my car would take me across the Mississippi River, through the Badlands, into the Rockies, and out of the High Desert, arriving finally to hills at the edge of the Pacific Ocean, golden in late summer, where I would sublet a small apartment from the friend of a friend and begin my next life. That I could name the place, *San Francisco*, and had been asked to go there for work meant that no one would fault me for my leaving. I was thirty-one years old, healthy, and still reasonably flush with insurance money. I had someone else's home to squat in, and a reason besides death to continue living in the world.

I had lived in Indiana with Ed and his family for a year and seven weeks. The night before I left, we went to dinner at the Italian restaurant. We drank expensive cocktails and ordered the specials. I made a toast and picked up the bill, fought back tears and tried the usual small jokes, and of course, it didn't feel like nearly enough of a gesture of thanks, and nothing at all like an end. For every new way we had imagined to say good-bye that summer, from the impromptu mall photo booth visit to the movie-plex binge on romantic comedies and space epics to our last-last trip to Baskin Robbins, in letters and collages and a terrific block party where neighbors inscribed with good wishes a *Far Side* anthology while we mixed cocktails in a cake mixer and sang the back catalog of Billy Joel, the prospect of my absence seemed only to stunt the emotional asymptotes, lengthening our days as we approached my departure date. Surely, we agreed, un-tacking the wall calendar and boxing my books, I wasn't *really leaving*. All this time, I think we meant, I hadn't only been their sad interloper.

All summer, I had sent letters and packages to a post office in the Sierras. Cait lived in San Francisco, but she was spending the summer at her family's cabin. We were old friends from the Peace Corps. Cait had come to our wedding and, three years later, to Katie's funeral. In the first months after Katie's death, Cait had mailed care packages from the Bay Area: sourdough bread, Pride pins, a *Hang in There, Kitty* picture book, a jar of fog. "This jar smells like mustard," my niece had said, frowning. A few weeks later, she swiped it from my desk and stuck it under her bed. Now, a carpenter named Dave was rebuilding the cabin deck. Sometimes when I called in the middle of the day, he and I would talk about the marmot slowly eating its way through the cabin walls or the free movie playing that week at the firehouse. When Cait called back in the evenings, I would disappear into the back room or yard. Some nights, I walked to the end of the subdivision and back, home and back again, running down the details of my day, the last hours since we had spoken, listening to her voice as the streetlights came on in sequence and around corners, lighting the path through the park where, on the Fourth of July, I held my finger in my ear and watched the sky hold the shapes of electric flowers that changed colors as their centers disappeared. Cait said she liked the print of the Barton Hays strawberries that I had sent from the

Indianapolis Museum of Art. So there really *was* fruit in the Midwest. Had I read *Cannery Row* yet? After our good-bye dinner, at a bar down the street, I drank beer with Ed and his friend. It was muggy, even for August. Water beaded our pint glasses. We talked about mountain biking, rock climbing, road trips, and finally, California. How long would I stay there? Where did I want to live next? I took the map out of my pocket and opened it on the table. We traced the route, agreeing it would be a beautiful drive, whether I went north through the Badlands, as I planned, or south through Kansas City, my hometown. South, we agreed, was probably faster. North would have the better trails. Before last call, we drank a shot of Katie's favorite whiskey. Through the window of the bar, the cars lit up, shook off the rain, and disappeared. The family that had taken me in and loved me after the great tragedy of my life, entirely and without hesitation, would tomorrow head back to school. In a few weeks, my room off the garage would become again the office.

The next morning, I made breakfast and drove my nieces to the bus. They waved from their seats, crowding near the back, smiling and waving. Wasn't this my year of grief and tragedy, as I had planned it, finally coming to its end? Already, the parents of the other children on the bus had gone back inside their houses. The street was quiet. Even my hybrid engine, idling, did not turn over. I watched the bus to the end of the block, where its hazards stopped flashing. The safety stop closed shut. The driver made a wide turn out of the subdivision. I pressed a button, pulled a lever into gear, and rolled silently through the light.

\*

As the car picked up speed, my body felt lighter. I could not quite name the feeling: nostalgia, but also a familiar resolve, tinged with frustration, to push on and past and through. With Lucinda Williams, I passed Lafayette. Katie had always called Ed from the Purdue University overpass to say that we were less than an hour away from Indianapolis. Past Remington, I cued up the Judds, Susan Werner,

Randy Travis: three hours of freight traffic and soy fields, truck stops
with diners, and the Tippecanoe war memorial, all the way to Hobart,
the one last small-big town east of the Skyway where, four years earlier,
Katie and I had married.

I hadn't been back to the County Line Orchard since, though it
occurred to me, as I passed the retro-chic gold-mirrored façade of
the Radisson, bronzing the highway with its long shadows, that I
might go one last time. The place would be quiet out of season; in
the middle of the week, almost certainly between weddings, with
no apple blossoms pasting the ground and no show tractors baling
hay. But the lacquered trellis in the loft of the barn, wrapped in tea
lights, might look again at least as quaint as I remembered it. The
stain on the wood would still dull the rafter lights. A year after the
wedding, Katie had sent the wedding planner two deep-dish pizzas
from Gino's East, frozen and packed in dry ice, delivered by private
driver, to say thank you for making the day beautiful and memorable.
It had cost us, what, a hundred dollars? The gesture had seemed so
extravagant. Katie had thought of it right away: the planner's favorite
Chicago haunt. Did she live still in the house down the road? Did she
know about Katie's death? Would she at least remember the pizza?
There was a clearing about halfway through the orchard where the
owners staged antique tractors. With me in ridiculous two-tone Doc
Martens and the elegant suit my father had picked out, Katie and I
had taken our wedding photos there. Twined with branches and run
through the machines with purple and green ribbons—our wedding
colors—the place, in memory, might again seem the beginning of a
long and happy life.

*Widower.* All year I had hated the word. I tried not to use it in
conversation. For a while I had even insisted: *widow. Widow* seemed
more quietly distinguished. Thinking I misunderstood the conven-
tion, someone had written after the funeral to say that I was misusing
*widow* by not adding the *-er.* I shot back an impromptu near-thesis
about the virtues of gender neutrality in a liberal age, as though any
sense of the political governed my reluctance to join the world's team

of failed husbands. Really, I hated how collective and indistinct the word made us, as though I had only to stand at the wall and welcome the next hysterical sap to say that this was how it was now. A part of our life was over. We had not stopped its ending.

I-465 made a circle around Indianapolis. All year, it had been my rim-and-spoke way station to the world, the place from which I could leave for a time and go anywhere else, before gradually drifting back. Always, I came back. I had only to pick an exit, drive fast, and when I was done—tired, or lonely, or simply feeling I had run out the clock—I raced back to my beautiful and temporary home, where I felt loved and safe. I had mostly gone east that year, to see friends and family. I had been to Vermont and back, Virginia and back, Ohio, Pennsylvania, and New York City, and always, back to Indiana. I knew the sequence of exits from the interstate in both directions by their neon signs: Gas & Food, Mega Shops, A Better Tomorrow. At the northernmost exit, the numbers reset. A short ramp doglegged into pasture and industrial farms. The larger interstate merged from all sides, pointing in one direction toward Ohio, the other toward Illinois.

Through construction lanes I followed heavy trucks overfilled with gravel. Every few miles, our logjam broke, and a fine dust of pellets rattled my windshield, blowing a sour tang of coal and fire through the vents. Fields on both sides of the interstate were green, still, but at the end of the season the color had dulled a little. The corn had begun to split. Could I really stop here and still leave Indiana? All year, I had wanted to stop. I had told myself I would do it. Now, I did nothing and waited. Already, I was past the orchard. Merrillville was a blur. Hobart was miles back. I kept pace with the luxury sedans and sports cars. They knew to watch for cops. A few lengths back, I matched their speed for a mile or so, but always, the faster cars opened the gaps between exits and quickly sped away.

\*

At Katie's funeral, I had wanted so much to stake out immediately for the West, to buy a car, disappear into the Rockies, and arrive somewhere I had never before visited, where no one I met would know Katie and where I had no part in any past that belonged to someone else. *California.* It was a plan that formed so neatly in my mind, and so manically sidestepped the obligations I felt in the moment to Katie's memory and her family, the funeral, the past, and our life generally, that I didn't trust it. I tried not to even think about it as we set the readings for the mass, dressed her body, and sat out on the back porch telling stories with strangers who had known Katie for longer than I had. And yet, in the nature preserve, after we spread her ashes, the plan returned. I imagined hills lined with trees and mountains near lakes, with open fields where everything anyone loved to eat grew year-round. I thought how unlike the rural Midwest all the places that Katie and I had chosen to live together were: Bangladesh, green all summer, until it became the season of rain, like Miami but more tropical and cooler at night, far from all that concrete that made Bucharest gothic and gray and temperate, its nearby mountains dotted with freshwater lakes between valleys, a long and perpetual season approaching spring that never seemed to settle as the extremes of midwestern winter and summer settled, though Bucharest was as much a city as Chicago would ever be, the heart of a region and for miles the only city that tourists bothered to name. Why had we never gone west across our own country? Someone had said before the funeral that there was a chance of rain that night. Rain would soak into everything and make the place green and bright. I thought how Katie would have liked becoming so quickly the place we had chosen for her, in a big field, almost an equal distance between her mother's house and her grandmother's house. It was a place I could always imagine visiting.

It seemed that I stood a good while by Katie's ashes. The afternoon heat was finally breaking. The sun was lower in the sky. I could hear cars on the state highway, nearly rush hour, with the first traffic coming past the lights at the state line. I started back up the path, and as I did so, I could not see the group. Surely, I thought, they were there, walking the trail back to their cars. We had agreed to meet for dinner at a shanty-themed restaurant facing the Chain O' Lakes. It would be our Illinois Catholic take on an Irish wake. No speeches, but chicken fingers with draft beer, flat-screened televisions, and an alt-country jukebox. We would leave the nature preserve and gather again later, though what seemed clear to me as I stood alone near her ashes was the creeping certainty that everyone had already gone, returning to families and homes and lives that waited to take them back, into which they might continue to carry Katie's memory, as they had known her, with or without me. What I felt was shame: that the service had been no good, that I had picked the wrong place for Katie, that the preserve was too remote to visit regularly and, without a marker, we would never again find the exact spot. I wanted instead a place to remind me exactly of where and how Katie had died. I feared forgetting it. And weren't Katie's ashes clumped too high on the ground to soak through?

Perhaps it occurred to me for the first time, then: I had no idea how to get from Illinois to California, or where I might stop on my way. I knew I would not return to Romania or Bangladesh or Chicago or Miami, but where exactly was I headed next? Already, I had a pile of letters, an in-box filled with emails, phone calls I had sent straight to voicemail that I could not bear to think of returning. After the local priest had given his lackluster eulogy for Katie, my sister-in-law's mother had called him personally to chew him out. He said he was sorry that he could not do better. She said she was sorry that he had not tried. I was grateful for such attention. I wanted to be the object of anyone's advocacy. I did not want to feel loved forever in sympathy. And yet, I wondered. Who would welcome my grief and look also with me beyond it?

I don't remember when I heard footsteps on the gravel. Someone was crossing from the clearing in the preserve. He might have stood there a good while watching me. The road ran nearly a half mile to the parking lot. Not a man but two friends turning the corner from the trail. My old friend Don stood on one side of me. Cait stood on the other. We made together a kind of sad lean at the place, into me but also with the slight suggestion, not quite a nudge, that we should step lightly away, catch ourselves, and begin in any direction, if only to catch up a little to the rest of the group. We walked like that very slowly, listening to the cars and the birds in the trees, of which there were so few as to constitute entirely an invention of song, a soundtrack to our unspectacular progress that we lacked a band to strike, until finally we saw them. What was it, maybe fifty people who had come to spread Katie's ashes? Everyone was there, on the far path to the parking lot, walking in twos and threes, not so far away at all. I thought, *I'm a part of that. I can still be a part of that.* It was a little more than a mile's walk. The path itself meandered as the full distance came gradually into view and then grew smaller by half, and half again. Katie's family was at the front of the group, nearly to the entrance. My family walked at the back, more slowly.

Three adjacent municipal baseball fields shared the parking lot. Lights on the diamond were warming up for the evening games, mostly dim bulbs still but a few brighter ones shining through the dusk. Simple patterns, the day's first constellations. It had been so easy, all week, to make small talk, but in my relief to find a group there, in my gratitude to see my two friends, what could my strange ambition to leave Indiana mean to anyone else? I said the first thing that came to mind. *California.* I tried to smile. I hated imposing like that. I hated needing anyone's sympathy. Years later, Cait would tell me that Don, so often irreverent, had asked her that night to make sure that I kept my promise. When the time was right, he told her, Cait should get me to California, if only for a quick visit. She agreed she would try to do it.

*

I can only describe the beginning, and try to describe it honestly—to narrow down the exact moment that an affection between Cait and me took root, and then name it, even if I'm not sure where that beginning really is. Was it that afternoon in the nature preserve? Was it six months later, when I flew out for Don's California weekend, corralling old friends for dinners and walks across the city, only talking about Katie, hardly myself, heartsick for Indiana? Was it that same afternoon sixteen years ago that I had met Katie, when she and Cait and Don and I were all new Peace Corps volunteers together, standing in a circle in a hotel ballroom in Seattle, playing icebreakers and scanning the room for some sense of what the next two years might make us into, and with whom we might become it?

What sticks in my memory now is a different afternoon. Late March. Almost nine months to the date after Katie had died. I have driven from Indiana to O'Hare Airport, on my way to visit my brother for the weekend. I am picking up Cait during her seventeen-hour layover, San Francisco to Chicago to Marrakech. Already, I know that I am moving to San Francisco that fall. Grief doesn't feel quite so desperate still. On a whim, Cait calls to say that I should show her my beloved adopted city, which becomes instead a long picnic at my favorite spot on the lakefront, followed by a walk across campus. I drop her off at the airport to make her connection. She is flying halfway around the world to hike across Morocco with an ex-boyfriend. And yet I feel so happy for the day. Some incantation I refuse to say out loud. *The future?* No, that's not right. I protest, again and again. *I will have no interest in Cait, in anyone at all, in fact, until at least one year after Katie's death.* I mean to keep my chaste year with all the vigilance of the cloister. Still, I know, one day, it will only technically be true. However I still feel like Katie's husband, I want to love again.

In May I make my second trip to San Francisco. Cait is sort of dating my friend but sort of not. I stay in her apartment. In every way I can think to do so, I mean simply to remain present and hope for the best. Here is the tension I have not anticipated, not between Katie and Cait, or Indiana and California, but between the inevitable present moment of grief, which seems nearly at times to remit, and the uncertain future, into which any feeling might arrive to take its place. That future—however wonderful or awful, charmed or fated or blank—means to come all at once and, if I refuse it, may dissolve just as quickly back into nothing. Or so I believe. Really, I have no idea what it might mean to actually love again. The prospect is terrifying. It is absolutely thrilling.

"A double-minded man is unstable in all his way." James said that, about the gap between faith and charity. In California I walk my widower's walk one last time. I stand at the window in Cait's kitchen, watching the city. The light behind me makes a darkness. I know that Katie would have shrugged her shoulders and smiled at what I want to do. She would have reminded me that life is short, the world is precious, and wasn't I the one who was always insisting that things like love and marriage last forever, that the heart is faithful and does not change? It certainly does not follow its whims; no, it distinguishes small affections from the stuff of true devotion. Katie knew that I didn't know better. I think maybe she loved me for it.

*

It happened like this. It was May. I was visiting California, supposedly looking for an apartment to rent that fall. After a long night of drinking and talking about therapy and politics and Chicago music festivals, I made out with Cait's roommate in the small guest room off her kitchen. We had stayed up late talking with her friends, then alone as we made pancakes, and after everyone else had gone home or to bed, we had danced to a song on the radio that she liked and I had kissed her. A few hours later, it was nearly morning. The whole Bay Area was sleeping through the end of a terrific heat spell. I had left the door to her room open to circulate the air. Cait was an early riser.

"Won't this be weird," the roommate said, "when Cait comes into the kitchen and sees us lying here?"

Cait and I had spent the day at her family home on the campus of the university where I would work that fall. I had met my new boss. I had bought a t-shirt with the name of the school printed on the front, and also a book of elegies by a famous poet. We had eaten dinner with Cait's extended family, and when dinner had gone late, we had called her roommate to cancel our plans to all go salsa dancing. The whole drive home, I had stewed. Why hadn't Cait taken her boyfriend on the all-day family tour that didn't end in salsa dancing? What did I need with third aunts and fifth cousins if I wasn't even the boyfriend, Cait's boyfriend, who probably *was* salsa dancing with someone— with anyone—at that very moment?

"Weird," I said to the roommate, "how?"

"You two have this history," she said, "and I think Cait likes you. So, her feelings might get hurt."

"Cait likes me?" I said. The room was brighter now. The morning trams were running. "But she's dating him."

"John," the roommate said, smiling and looking right at me. "I mean, there's dating, and then there's *dating*."

I jumped out of bed and raced across the kitchen to Cait's room. I checked the clock on the oven: 6:37 a.m.

"Is it okay if . . ." I said, waving my arms and nodding my head at Cait's door.

The roommate laughed.

"You go get 'em, Tiger," she said.

*I should go to bed,* I told myself as I knocked on her door. I was supposed to leave in a couple of hours for my friend's graduation from journalism school.

"Cait," I said, whispering through the door, "I was just making out with your roommate and I told her that I liked you and she told me that you liked me, too, so I think we need to talk."

Cait opened the door, confused, and asked if anyone had drowned. She had been dreaming that we—Cait, the roommate, and me—had all crashed together in a plane into the ocean. Now, she was sitting on the bed. She was wearing pajamas with a full collar that opened across her shoulders, showing high on her pale skin freckles, her long hair pulled to one side as she gathered herself at the edge of the bed, reaching out to hold my hand, fixing me with her blue eyes, a darker blue than Katie's, her voice even, practical and full of feeling, her hands warm and steady. She liked me too. Of course, she liked me. But didn't other things matter more right now, like Katie and the death anniversary? What about Katie? she asked. Didn't I think it would be weird because of Katie? Wasn't it all too soon? Cait didn't want to be my consolation prize, and certainly not my rebound. She liked me too much for that. Maybe, she said, that fall, after I was settled, after I had left Indiana and found my own place in the city—maybe then, yes, we could take things slowly. I seemed sad, still, not so fragile but maybe not yet entirely whole. We were old friends, and who knew how these things worked after knowing each other for so long? And what if there was no chemistry? She liked me, yes, but this wasn't "like" we were talking about, not if we both meant what we seemed to be saying. And was that my moment then, I thought, to lean in and kiss her, whatever she was saying, to whisk away all the doubt and intervening time we agreed was so important and to be bold? I couldn't do it. It was all such good news, I told myself, and I couldn't bring myself to ask the question I wanted to ask, not of myself, and certainly not of Cait, because I wasn't sure it would be true unless I said it out loud. *Even when I was married to Katie?* And what did that matter, now, whether it was true or not? What mattered was that I liked Cait *now*. I liked Cait a great deal, and I wanted to do something about it.

\*

A few hours later, my friend crossed the dais. The heat spell broke. I borrowed a jacket from a friend of a friend and caught an early ride back to the city, and when I got to the apartment, Cait was already asleep. I went to her door and thought about knocking again. Instead, I took a sleeping pill, pulled the room up over my shoulders, and waited for it to disappear.

Cait was up first thing. She had already gone out to buy us muffins and coffee. Through the doorway, I could see her, busy in the kitchen. The roommate, Cait said, had left for the weekend. We sat together in the kitchen, making small talk, and all the time I wondered, should I say it again? Had I said something wrong? She gave me a hug good-bye and told me to call her to let her know I'd made it back safe to Indiana. I took the train to the airport. All the good feeling and certainty I had held inside of me since our talk the morning before seemed now uncertain and spent, merely magical, a spell against Indiana whose words I was already forgetting, a feeling too bright and happy and eager to overwhelm the rest of my life. I found my car, loaded my bags, and sat in the front seat, waiting. For a while, there was nothing, though I could feel it coming on all morning and afternoon. I knew all the signs, and when finally the spark seemed more than hysterical, it was still another part of grief: great, heaving sobs so full of fear and feeling that, when they finally stopped, I couldn't move and my left ear was clogged and I didn't hear anything out of it for days.

*You fucking idiot,* I thought. *341 days.*

*A year,* I kept telling myself, *you couldn't even wait a full fucking year.* Already, a migraine was starting. I hadn't had one in months. I put my jacket over my head to make the space in front of my eyes dark and simple. Flashes of light spun across my vision, in larger and larger circles that slowly dissolved into nausea and pain. Half-blind, fumbling at the phone, I called my therapist and asked if she could schedule a session that afternoon. I took a different pill, tilted my seat all the way back, and waited for the first gap of missed time, then the next, to accumulate into an absence of thinking and feeling. I lost count of the gaps. A few hours later, I snapped out of something that wasn't quite sleep. I felt a little less manic, more a part of everything, though I knew that that was a haze too. Still, I could at least drive. I paid a fee to leave the airport. I drove across Indianapolis to the therapist's office and sat in a different parking lot, checking my phone for messages from Cait, or the roommate, or my friend, listening to the radio and counting down the time until my session began.

\*

East of Gary, Indiana, the sky filled with smog, or industrial steam, or whatever sanctioned waste left the stacks and yellowed the afternoon sky as it rose into the clouds and disappeared over Lake Michigan.

The pollution, everyone seemed to agree, wasn't nearly as bad as it looked. The pale, sickly glow had something to do with the relative position of the sun, humidity levels, the width of the lake, the temperature and gravity and science enacting all manner of illusion on my fragile cortexes. Really, Gary was the part of Indiana that Chicago had long ago claimed as its buffer, a place where good things could happen to one city, whatever bad things it did to the people who lived in the other city. What Gary looked like was the beginning of the end of civilization. On either side of Gary, the air was clean and the sky was blue.

Driving into Gary felt sometimes like discovering a secret history, a past from which there were no clear exits. Businesses were scarce. Exits were marked for landmarks: the independent and unaffiliated minor league baseball team; the historic downtown; a rusted plate tacked under each mile marker, acknowledging again and again Michael Jackson's birthplace. The plates always gave me a minor thrill. The city's sense of Michael Jackson seemed to begin with *Off The Wall* and end with *Dangerous*: twelve years of iconography, swagger, and pop, all promise and no decline. Gary's sense of itself was correspondingly narrow and epic. On that stretch of interstate, one sign after the next reminded me, I was passing The Magic City, The City of the Century, The Steel City [Birthplace of Michael Jackson]. Gary had an ivy-covered courthouse, dune beaches, nine parks, and three professional sports franchises, but all that anyone passing through ever saw or seemed to remember were the smokestacks.

I had received on my phone, all year, daily reminders to send money to political organizations. John McCain was ready to name his vice presidential nominee. The Supreme Court's conservative majority hated women, minorities, justice, and the planet itself. My five more dollars were all that stood between Rapture and Progress. Here was our new democracy: collecting more money than the old entrenchments, in one- to twenty-dollar increments. Email subject lines addressed me by name. Celebrities thanked me for victories. With each successive message, our good fight felt at least as much like grandstanding as a fair contest. How were we measuring our eventual victory except by what we did not win? Everything was in play: the White House, Congress, a few state houses, our city comptroller, a municipal district special ombudsman. And after that, nature, the world, the idea of America in that world, the future of space. Wouldn't it send quite a message if the Dakotas turned a rich bipartisan purple; if every congressional district north of the Allegheny and west of Carson City was dark blue, and if we then, for good measure, also passed a referendum protecting a ground rodent? All summer, Cait and I had talked about Katie. How could we not?

In letters and phone calls, at grocery stores and restaurants, across highways and long hikes, I told stories about places I had traveled—*we* had traveled. Cait asked questions. She listened to my answers. I was, in those conversations, direct and honest. Cait tried not to offer the usual consolations. I was grateful for that. I knew that I had never been so honest with someone, even Katie; that, if I could have been so honest, under any other circumstances, I would have guarded away at least my shame. With Cait, there was power in disclosure. I could say the things I wanted in a life now. I did not worry about distinctions between widower (reverent, careful, polite) and friend (disclosing, intimate, honest). Cait and I were older and more frank, more clear-minded than our former Peace Corps selves, and more certain of who we were and what we wanted. Always, I tried not to make a defense. Like a spell, or an especially complicated recipe, the thing we revealed together, careful step by step, held an unmistakable shape. Once we recognized it, we took pride in the final stages. It seemed inevitable and nearly complete.

Crossing the interstate, parallel with the consumptive stacks, I could hardly make out the golden dome in the city's center. Once, Gary, Indiana, had seemed an idea, a lost ideal, the end of the end of a beginning. And yet, here was Gary, still. I loved the city for its refusal to acknowledge the obvious fact of its decline, for the pride by which it lived in a present moment, celebrating the past, celebrating the future, and never quite explaining what had happened in between.

To anyone who bothered to look around or ask, the government was semi-functioning at best. City coffers were empty. The population had more than halved in thirty years. But whoever lived in Gary seemed still to love it. They voted to put sunshine and rainbow piping on the dented city signs, sprucing up the home of a defunct record company, claiming the world's biggest pop star, whatever the state of his decline. Decades after the King of Pop had left town and headed west, Gary seemed still to exist at the end of one dream, ready for another. However reciprocated, it cheered on whoever was passing through. I was grateful for the acknowledgment. I wouldn't want to leave the state of Indiana going any other way.

*

The therapist's office was only a few blocks from Ed's house, in a lot that some developer must have imagined before the recession would fill with trees and become a park. For now, the low-rise offices in the lot were empty. The parking lot was empty too. There was halting construction across the street, a mess of yellow and rusting hulks that seemed never to move, though they periodically made such a terrific noise during our sessions that we had to stop and close our eyes, wait for the silence and begin again. I didn't particularly like the room. It was not the quiet bungalow-style nook where we had begun our work a year earlier. No children's artwork or sagging bookshelves framed the therapist's various degrees. I could reach nearly across the room from my office chair. My savior, oracle, seen-your-kind-before-and-will-again trauma specialist, whose shrewd sensibility encompassed everything except surprise, was only renting the new space to close out work with her last few patients. She was moving to Florida in July. I should call her any time, and also meet her doctor friend in Chicago on my way out of town to see if I liked the fit. Since she recommended him, I imagined I would like the Chicago doc. But I couldn't imagine staying in touch with her, much less calling her at home in Florida.

Right away, she didn't like the sound of Cait. What was Cait doing, dating my friend if she meant to love me? Was Cait always so dishonest? Dishonest people tended to break hearts. Would Cait break my heart? Had I thought about how well I *really* knew my old friend? The roommate sounded grounded and reliable. If I should date anyone, then the roommate was a good person to start with. And hadn't we agreed, the therapist continued, that I would take things very slowly after Katie's death, and enjoy these last few months in Indiana, the chance to say good-bye not only to Katie's brother and his family, but also, a way of making a life, that life of grief that would not last forever—that was, already, clearly not lasting?

Worse than wanting to fall in love with Cait, I realize now, I was committing the cardinal sin of the psychoanalytic devout. I was explaining something I did not particularly want to understand. It was a distinction I was making more and more often in sessions: that life and this one, that place and here, then and now. It was terrifying to think that everything I had pursued in the course of a year's work in therapy was perhaps now at risk of a faltering attention to the future. "You might even meet someone you've never met before," the therapist said, "and maybe that would be simpler too?"

The therapist had a habit of rattling the bracelets on her wrist. They were turquoise. There was no turquoise in Florida. Turquoise came from the Southwest, north to California. It was a by-product of copper mining at one end of a mountain range, picked out of the stone pile and shipped to remote places, where it was polished and strung together in jagged shapes, with accents of howlite, blackstone, opal, and jasper to make the blue shine. *Oh,* I told myself, *I know the kind of people who wear turquoise jewelry.* Touchy-feely chanters. Fans of harmonics who, in circles, intoned. I hated that the therapist wore turquoise. I hated that she did not like Cait. Of course, it was her job not to like Cait. She didn't *really* have an opinion about Cait, one way or the other. She was testing my assumptions. She was treating her patient. She was doing the tail end of work from which she was retiring, and knowing the ethical obligation not to leave a patient in crisis, she felt comfortable enough with our work to let me know it was near its end.

I wanted our work to continue. I wanted to be in California with Cait right then, as the clock ticked down the end of our session in Indiana, the one I had called my therapist *in crisis* to arrange, and when it was time to go, what I felt was neither relief nor persecution. I did not gnash my teeth. The prospect of a cure lingered, hopeful as ever, with a next session. For now, like turquoise, grief worked into shape and around other things. Cait. California. Moving. Work. Leaving Indiana. The stuff that came after trauma did not interest the therapist. Certainly, it would not disrupt her life and summer plans. Here was the actual epiphany, and I had missed it entirely. For weeks now, we had begun to work on something far more ordinary and complicated than grief and trauma and loss. I was arguing for a life partner, about suitability and temperament, character and grace and chance. I was imagining bakeries and traffic patterns, courtships, earthquakes, and selves. We were talking about who might help me to best make the transition to living in a new city, where I would do new work and begin to make a new life. In other words, we were no longer talking about Katie. Probably, we hadn't talked about her for quite some time.

*

At the last toll plaza before the Chicago city limits, I bought a coffee and cued up Bruce Springsteen's *The Rising*. I had listened to the album all year, every trip, the whole way through, until it became a superstition, the thing I had to do before I finally left Indiana. Again, I rolled down the windows and cranked the volume. A friend had burned *The Rising* for Katie and me to listen to on our drives from Miami to my parents' home in Central Florida. Then, it had been our somber gem. Every song promised that things were getting better, if only because they couldn't get any worse. Most of the time, after the first few songs, Katie would change albums or turn off the radio all together. *The Rising* was meant to exhaust. Katie had little tolerance for purposeful exhaustion, however moving the music or cathartic the occasion. "Life is hard enough," she would say, "without Bruce Springsteen." In Indiana

*The Rising* had been my mind-blowing, self-indulgent cathartic. I had yielded to its thrill. I had wanted the feeling to radiate past the limits of my body. I wanted everyone to hear the music.

I called my sister-in-law to say I might arrive in time to pick up my nephews from their preschool. I thought, *I should call Katie's mom too, and stop by the nature preserve.* I knew I wouldn't do it, not this time. I had any number of excuses. It was at least an hour and a half past Chicago to her house, and a good half hour past that to the nature preserve. Even if I beat the traffic, I would get stuck rubbernecking it back, all the while missing time with the boys, my brother and his wife, my friends, and all the places I meant to go one last time before setting out west. I wanted to see them all before I left. I did not want to spend my first night away from Indiana back in Katie's hometown.

Everything I owned was trunked under the hatchback with the seats folded down and the passenger seat pulled up; everything except for my bike, which I had fashioned with bungee cords to a simple frame. It was a trail bike, built for rivers and mountains: everywhere I did not want to go again after Katie's death. Katie had given me the bike four years earlier, for our first Christmas as a married couple. I had just had it tuned up. I had ridden it across Indianapolis all summer, listening to podcasts and stopping, at my farthest points out, to call Cait and talk about anything, everything, sometimes just to hear her voice. Now, on hills and across potholes, I could hear the thump of the front wheel on the plastic bumper. It rattled there a few seconds, just long enough to call attention to itself, however fast I drove, whatever I was listening to, and then it was silent for the next stretch of miles.

# Badlands

Chicago came east so fast I drove under as much as toward it, along as quickly as through it. Always it happened this way. At a distance, I admired the skyline. Up close, I followed a maze of exits, tunnels, and bridges to the north side of the city, half a mile from the lake and three miles from the apartment in Uptown where Katie and I had lived before we married. Then, we had gone over to my brother's townhouse on Fridays to play spades, order Thai food, and at the end, pass my baby nephew back and forth, read him stories, hide behind the sofa with his favorite stuffed animals, and sing his favorite songs. Now, I was arriving at Jeff's new place. I had grieved for Katie there. I had held out the phone for Jeff's wife, Sheila, to hear Cait's voicemails. On his fifth birthday, beneath two large trees, my nephew and I sat together trying to tune a toy guitar. His fingers were too small to make the shapes and the plastic pegs lost their tension quickly, but still, he liked holding the guitar and pretending to make it sing. Each time we did it, I thought of those evenings when Katie and I had met at the Old Town School of Folk Music, after her guitar classes, to walk to the park and practice barre chords. Like everything in Chicago that brought her to mind, the place was wrong, the time of day too early or late, the feeling a little too present. Still, I missed it: Katie, years alive yet, loving something new.

That first morning, we watched *The Wonder Pets* and played Candyland. We made pancakes and walked to the park. As my nephews climbed up and down the jungle gym next to a statue of Dorothy Gale, I called Cait and offered to buy her a plane ticket to meet me in Montana. On short notice, I said, the best I could do was to get her to Billings via Reno and Oakland, first thing on a Friday, three weeks out. We could visit Yellowstone and see the Great Salt Lake. We could even cross all of hot and flat Nevada. She laughed and agreed it sounded fun. She said she'd like to do it. *We're doing it,* I thought as I hung up the phone. *I did it.* The summerlong fantasy was now a plan.

While the boys napped, I walked to the apartment Katie and I had shared. I had mapped out the route to pass most of Katie's favorite haunts: the bakery that gave tours and free samples, the travel café with kitchen-sink cookies and a lending library, the model train museum–urban greenhouse next to the fifty-seat theater where we had seen on my birthday an early preview of a play about a music teacher who loved her student and taught him how to play the guitar. *Mrs. McKenzie's Beginner's Guide to the Blues* was amazing. We had never seen anything like it. We had subscribed to the theater company that night, and then to another, and had later signed up for a hip-hop dance class, volunteering at the neighborhood church, and of course, Katie's guitar classes. That was the year we decided to get out of the apartment more often. We were sick of always driving to Indiana to do it. Now, the bakery was under new ownership: no samples. The theater was closed, though the chain noodle shop across the street was just opening for the day. A man in a white shirt was wiping down tables near the window. It was too early still to eat.

"You're making a ritual," the new therapist said later that afternoon when we met in his Hyde Park office, "and rituals are always messy at first."

He had a habit of closing his eyes when neither of us was talking.

"You left Indiana."

I tried closing my eyes too.

"Now, you're deciding how to leave Chicago."

His office was filled wall to wall with books: shelves of books, stacks of books, books marked with bright stickies and opened to the page, books beneath framed prints from the Art Institute and the National Gallery, books in boxes on a small desk between two sofas where he charged various electronic devices, an electric tea kettle, a clip lamp attached to a hardcover edition of Mark Twain, dark blue along the spine, a little darker than the other books in the series, which were stacked like dominos all the way to the door, where they climbed both sides of the frame.

"This first time," he said, "maybe just try to take the best deal you can get. Sixty-five cents on the dollar. Seventy cents."

I could feel in the tightness of my own shoulders Katie's big shrug, equal parts indifference and exhaustion, a little annoyed.

"Really, John," she had said one night in Bucharest while we were washing dishes. "What do you think is going to happen if I die before you do?"

I told the therapist that I liked the dollar-and-change theory. I liked any theory about happiness that let me keep most of it. There I was, finally on my way to California, and I could hardly see my way to the end of a sentence that didn't name some new calamity between Chicago and Montana that might get in the way of my finding Cait: bears, thunderstorms, desert fever, Lyme-diseased ticks, lost highways that turned deeper and deeper between South Dakota stalactites and arrived to nowhere anyone I knew had ever left. Why couldn't I simply focus on that happiness and let the rest go by the wayside? It seemed irresponsible not to anticipate danger. I felt alarmist and even self-pitying for mentioning the danger first, before my eagerness to get to Cait.

The apartment building had been repainted, yellow trim on a light tan, which gave the effect of looking at something restored and made to look too young. I stood on Agatite Avenue for a few minutes, uncertain what more I should find in person that I hadn't all year imagined. Was the rooftop garden in season? Were the interior apartments three deep on one side still and four across? Katie and I used to sit in our corner windowsill counting families walking back from the lakefront. One night, we had watched a man try to convince a police officer that the prostitute in his car owed him change. They had left in separate cruisers, in a whir of silent lights. His car had sat parked out front all month. Now, the cars on the street were nicer: late-model Toyotas and Subarus and Volkswagens. Children in blue and white uniforms milled the new school park across the street. They climbed impatiently to the top of play structures, whooshing like hungry fish across an aquarium, falling into and around each other, smiling and laughing, frenzying their way back up. A teacher near the fence made eye contact and smiled. I looked away. No one else seemed to notice that I was standing there.

I took the shorter route back to Jeff's town house. Clark Street, a few blocks over, was busy and congested. Phalanxes of Cubs fans were making their way to and from the El, emptying and filling the bars near Wrigley, radiating disbelief. They had gone to see the Cubs almost win. The Cubs had nearly done it. Block after block, men in webbed caps hung out the sides of floor-to-ceiling windows, happily sun drunk and blurry, sweaty stalactites of testosterone bellowing Dave Matthews and David Gray at no one in particular, making of loneliness and frustration the same fraternal bond of inevitability that was loving the Cubs when they lost. *We all feel like that,* they seemed to say, *about a lot of things, buddy.* I didn't want to hear it. Katie had given me a Cubs t-shirt as a wedding present. It was our private joke, her gentle way of insisting that I try to enjoy myself, wherever I was, a little more. I had rooted mightily for the Cubs all year. *Assholes in Cubs t-shirts,* I thought now. *What do they know about suffering?* It felt small and superior to cross wide of them on the sidewalks. Still, I kept my distance. I plugged in my headphones, sweeping with each quick step mini-avalanches of red plastic cups.

*You're in the middle of a love story,* I told myself, *tell it to yourself like it's a love story.* A young widower and his old friend meet cute in a Montana airport. They drive together to California. They fall in love all summer, and when they meet in person, a second life begins for the widower. He is grateful for it. He loves that life all out of proportion to his past, and even to himself.

I liked that story. I trusted it, even as some part of the telling felt too deliberate, defensive even.

To whom was I making my account?

If I loved Chicago so much, why was I working so hard to miss it?

The therapist walked me to the door at the end of our session. He had parked his bike in the hallway, an old ten-speed with drop bars and a light frame. As we said good-bye, he put on a white helmet with a gray chinstrap. It scrunched his face together and made him look a bit like Lenin.

"Survival," he had said at the beginning of our session, "is entirely different from the stuff of daily living."

Through the window, I could see the giant Walgreens a few blocks over. Someone had pasted election posters to the side of the building, the Shepard Fairey design that was suddenly everywhere: HOPE repeating across parallel squares set one beside the next, three tall and maybe twenty across, at bright blue and red and white angles to the pale brick wall.

"Yeah," I said, "but what if I screw it up?"

He smiled and closed his eyes.

"Well," he said, "then we can talk about that too."

\*

The day after I bought Cait's ticket, Dad called to say that Grandma was hospitalized, in a coma. It was early still but indications were not good. The doctors thought she might die quickly, though it was possible that she could linger for weeks, a few months even. I packed up the car and said a hasty good-bye. I would see my brother and his family again in a few days in St. Joseph, Missouri, I was sure of it. Grandma had said for years that she hoped the Good Lord would send her another big stroke at night and be done with it. Now, it seemed, she had gotten her wish.

I called Cait from the road to say that she should hold on to the ticket and wait. She was so sorry, I should go, no worries, of course we'd figure it out. Iowa was green and beautiful west of the Mississippi River and south into Missouri. I had made the drive before with my mother a half dozen times, to and from Jeff's college in Peoria, Illinois, stopping in St. Joe on our way from Kansas City. Eighteen years later, farms and hills still rolled into one long pasture. Gas stations staggered the same few exits. The landmarks were either ironic or charming, I couldn't always be sure. Iowa was funny in that same way that everyone I knew from the Midwest liked to hold jokes and turn them, at the very last moment, into stories, daring the listener to miss a subtle punch line. "The Corn Palace: The World's Only Corn Palace." "The Future Birthplace of James T. Kirk." It felt good to drive such long stretches of the land at a time. There was no sense of scale to my progress, only periodic acceleration and braking and the low hum of the engine charging the battery to make more speed.

Grandma and I had talked nearly every week, a practice I had learned from Katie, who was her grandmother's namesake. When we were first dating, Katie had suggested I keep my chats with Grandma in the steady, middle range of not talking about anything for too long. The key, she had said, was quantity rather than quality. Call every week and say nothing. Mention the weather, work, news, school. It took a little less than an hour to cover the bases—which nurses were honest, whether I liked my work, the side effects of various drugs she worried meant she should stop taking them, the price of corn—and always, in the end, I felt that Grandma and I had caught up. In Indiana, especially, our chats about nothing in particular had accumulated into a short history, the year we had both spent living at a distance to the world. I was careful not to look too closely in those chats for a life after grief. At least as much as Grandma, I think, I was wary to hear a certain tone in my voice. And yet, beyond the small strokes and surgery after one kidney had stopped working, the checking in and out of hospitals for days, then weeks at a time, her slow decline had become, for us, a simple ritual of closeness. I called. More often than not, she picked up the phone.

*I don't want anyone else I love to die alone* wasn't the clearest logic. For one thing, Dad would arrive soon to keep vigil. Probably, he would get there before I did. He would have Mom for support, and they were good in a crisis. *I owe it to Grandma for flying out for Katie's funeral* was closer to what I really felt. In a wheelchair, paralyzed on her right side, forced to accept the charity of airline officials and an estranged sister, Grandma had never once invoked her self-pity in place of my sorrow. Even at the nature preserve, after the funeral mass, her hazel eyes sharp and her gray brow tucked under her silk scarf, tied properly even in that heat, she withheld any criticisms. To spread Katie's ashes after the mass was distinctly un-Catholic, but Grandma had said nothing against it. There was a sense of scale to her empathy that had surprised me, a light behind the darkness that seemed more than grief. Grandma had loved Katie. She had genuinely liked Katie too. For anyone else, Grandma's death would not follow Katie's. But I could do this last thing for Grandma. Whether or not she knew it—and following her stroke, there was no way to be sure she did—I would be there.

The hospital where Grandma was dying, where her husband had died fifteen years earlier and her mother ten years before that, was the only public hospital in the region for a good fifty miles. A row of squat buildings lit through each room and along the exterior pitched floodlights at a slight elevation to the fields around it. The effect was to see at first a baseball diamond, county fairgrounds, the state university: a placed filled with skilled people who required a lot of light to do exceptional things. Even the concrete was painted to look like white stone. Two signs moved traffic in opposite directions: into the visitor's parking lot at the front or along the new wing down the hill to the emergency bay. Bodies arrived and departed from a discreet berth. *Catholic,* I thought, *to the end.* Everyone was welcome to walk through the front door, so long as they first climbed the hill.

I parked near the entrance and stretched my legs. Seven hours driving: twenty-six minutes faster than the computer had predicted. It felt good to stand, better still to walk. The coffee was wearing off and I was hungry, but the hunger had a way of sharpening my senses, magnifying the need I felt to do something important. *Go inside already. See it for yourself.* I walked around the building to get my bearings. Somewhere close, I knew, was Dad's hometown, and beyond that, the city where I had lived for the first fourteen years of my life. Grandma was upstairs. Each time the automatic doors opened, a burst of cold air whipped out through the muggy heat. I signed my name at the desk and stuck an ID on my shirt. I followed the lines on the floor to the western bank of elevators, then out to the floor and wing, turning a short hallway toward a room where my parents sat on either side of the bed, holding Grandma's hands and praying.

*

We arrived mornings, first thing, for the doctor's rounds. We went back to the hotel for a late breakfast and rebooked flights. A representative for the airline offered to waive the cancellation fee if Dad mailed a copy of Grandma's death certificate. "But, she isn't dead," I said, trying to sound helpful. The manager kept our rooms indefinitely, on a discounted rate for family emergencies. "Except for holidays," she explained, "the place doesn't really fill." We thanked her for her hospitality. In an empty conference room off the lobby, we spread brochures on a table and checked what we thought we understood against what the Internet seemed also to explain. We spent long afternoons and evenings with Grandma, at first together and then in shifts, watching the Beijing Olympics on the in-room television. I tried to make small talk. "They like to know you're here," a nurse told me. *But isn't she brain-dead?* I wanted to ask, except I couldn't think of a nice way to ask it, and then, what if Grandma *had* heard me ask it?

One afternoon, over lunch, a specialist visited the room. Things were not progressing. The insurance company would pay for hospice care at an approved facility. There were three "homes" within five miles of the hotel. We left the hospital to meet with an administrator. We held interviews, signed applications, studied fact sheets, and checked for vacancies. Mom and I stood in hallways while Dad sat in one vacant room after another, trying to get a feel for how Grandma might live in the space and whether she would like it. After a while, he had a checklist. Was there a window view, sunlight, noise at night, a comfortable bed? A hospice care facilitator was assigned to our case. He wore bow ties and dragged his left leg when he walked. Every morning, he explained the latest deadline for each step of the pending transfer. He suggested that we wait each one out and not take them together. There was no point, he said, really, to working ahead; when the time came, we'd move Grandma, if it came to that, and it either would or wouldn't; we just had to wait. We waited like that for one week and the start of the next. In the last facility we visited, the hallways were filled with men attached to IVs, women in wheelchairs, someone lying half-awake on gurneys or holding an arm out to a nurse, oxygen tubes stuck up his nose. *No one would choose to come here to die*, I thought, and I couldn't help thinking of the room in the funeral home where the director had laid out Katie's body. *Of course, they don't. Someone chooses it for them.*

\*

Aunt Lillian, Grandma's youngest sister, came by in the afternoons to sit. We talked about the Cubs, California, Michael Phelps, the heat. She held out the back of my Kosuke Fukudome t-shirt and laughed. She thought his last name was an obscene pun. Lillian had doted on me as a boy. I had loved visiting her small ranch house with the giant satellite dish in the backyard of, what seemed to my youthful eyes, all of Kansas's corn and soybean fields, just out the porch window and under her husband's watchful eye. Lillian and Archie hosted Easter. She made terrific deviled eggs. She would always sneak me a few as she took the plastic wrap off the main dishes, before calling everyone in for supper. Aunt Lillian was the baby of her family too, several years younger than her other sister, Soph. She knew something about pecking orders. Lillian's smile lingered with little of her sisters' sadness. I wasn't allowed to do so very often, but I spent a few nights on her farm, sleeping in my third cousin's room. I have always romanticized rural life on a working farm because of it.

Archie died the year I graduated from college, on his tractor in a field. The neighbors came out to help finish the harvest and get everything to market. A local newspaper ran an article about it, with a picture of folding tables in the field topped with hot plates, and men standing around drinking coffee and smiling. I knew Archie as the gruff cardplayer who sat in his recliner after supper drinking beer and watching the Lions play the Cowboys or the Royals play the Tigers, though much later, I saw something of his mischief too. At my grandparents' fiftieth wedding anniversary, he leaned over to my sister and me as they cut the cake, smiled, and whispered, "That's the first time in fifty years I've seen them kiss each other."

"I feel him there sometimes," Lillian said to me one afternoon as I walked her to the elevator. Older now, even when she smiled, she looked so much like Grandma. "I'll be lying in bed and having a dream, or I'll wake up from a dream, and there he is, right next to me. I don't mean—no, no—just—I know he's there. And I'll start talking to him about this or that, and he'll listen."

She smiled at me.

"It must happen to you too," she said. "You must miss Katie and get awfully lonesome."

I wanted to agree with her. I did miss Katie. I did get lonesome. I might even notice it in dreams about Katie, how they were very different from those in which she didn't appear. But did I ever wake thinking Katie was next to me? No, that never happened.

"I sometimes dream she's there," I said, wanting to meet Lillian halfway. I wanted to tell her all about Cait, and all of the happiness I could not wait to find in Montana. I wanted to say that I was falling in love. Again. "But I really don't think she is."

Lillian smiled again and hugged me. I could smell the powder on her skin, rosewater, as she kissed me on the cheek.

"She's there, John," she said, "whether you know it or not."

\*

"It's time," the nurse said over the phone that last morning. Dad made his way to the hospital quickly and I came later. There was neither haste nor coldness in anyone's manner. No one panicked or tried to stop the inevitable. I felt separate of that work. We held hands. Dad prayed. I stood outside the room while Dad and Mom went in, and after a while, the nurses came and went, a doctor, a medical officer, a police officer, and eventually, even, the coroner. All in a couple of hours, neither rushed nor overly deliberate, but rather, following a schedule, Grandma's death was witnessed and accounted for, and yet, in the end, for all its pacing and deliberation, this death was nothing like Katie's. Or, it was like Katie's in the broad sense that I was there and, just after the fact, the interventions of strangers came fast enough to make familiar the unreason of death and, then, to dismantle all of its attendant architecture—stripping the bed, removing the effects, bleaching the equipment and room—until it seemed that the room was reset and that no one had ever stayed in the room before, and certainly, no one had lived there at the end of any life. Otherwise, nothing changed.

\*

On the way to the funeral, my sister and I stopped at Grandma's apartment. The room was as I remembered it from my visit that spring: two green easy chairs from the old house now set by the window with white towels on the headrests, a coffee table, a television with a box remote. All of it was meticulously ordered and, in its own way, spartan, showing nothing more than what day to day she had needed and could not get from the nursing home staff, at the cafeteria, or in the common rooms. At first glance, the cupboards were sparse— cornflakes, salt and pepper, decaffeinated tea—though, on closer inspection, Grandma had kept a high shelf stocked at the far back with hundreds of pills, of every shape and color, round pills and oblong pills and tabs, half and quarter doses, in the original plastic blisters or under the orange stoppers with her name, the dosage, and instructions printed down one side and up the next. The pills were crammed into the space, a store of what she would need one day far in excess of what she might ever use: stacks of old pennies, expired credit cards, the Soviet nuclear arsenal. How closely, I thought, that shelf resembled the cellar she had stacked to the ceiling with preserves, a near wall of green bean jars that Katie and I had finally thrown out, labeled with Scotch tape and dated far too many years too late to eat, the pounds of butter smashed into the deep freezer next to the frozen juice, tubs of whipped topping, and sides of beef. We had chipped the freezer ice to liberate and name the last pieces. We hardly recognized what Grandma had dug in. She stocked up, yes; there was no denying it. She hated to have too little of anything. Really, I think, she hated pain more than she liked pleasure. Or, she hated the idea of pain and ever being unready for it more than she liked the idea of avoiding it. Pain proved something that no other feeling could test: courage, but also the ability to withstand the worst, to suffer with dignity, to make a space in oneself for what others by habit avoided or tried to avoid. Grandma guarded cautiously against being made to feel strong or weak. Perhaps the pills were a kind of makeshift sanctuary, a shelf too high to ever reach. Seeing them all in one place, I felt humble and weak. No one could survive on such provisions. My sister and I took mementos from the apartment. Grandma had always stocked the candy dish for our arrivals with spice drops. Along the sides, the dish was carved into elaborate ridges, nearly crystal, except the edges were sharp and the top, as I twirled it on the table, made no music. Glass. *I'll take it,* I thought, *and it won't be empty.* From the cupboard I took down a few bottles and rolled the pills in the glass.

That night, we took a driving tour of the city in Dad's rental car. One last time, we crammed as a family into a sedan. Our adult selves still held the space of our designated seats with all the adolescent marking out of territories. We bumped elbows and giggled. We started at the childhood home on the south side and made our way north and west to the ranch-style house with the steep yard. From the curb, it seemed unchanged: two windows, green shutters, the short porch, the empty lot once a garden where Granddad kept his store before it burned down. Who knew what the new owners had done with the rooms inside. I could still imagine Grandma and Granddad in that kitchen, just married, arguing, according to family legend, about money. Granddad says that he wants his own business in St. Joe, clear and outright, and that his father will stake him to start it. Grandma is too proud to take anyone's charity, but she likes the idea of owning a business. She is a nurse at the state hospital. When she does dishes, she fills the sink with an inch of water: more than enough. Out the window, the neighbors are building a deck that reaches all the way to the property line. If they take the money, she thinks, will that be the end of it? Meaning, have they gotten as much as they should? Can they get more? And I have to hear it in her voice, so many years later, that first inkling of a resentment that she will nurse the rest of her life, before any other. *What do they take us for, anyway?*

\*

Katie and I had helped Grandma move out of that house and into the nursing home. There were boxes lined to one side of the dining room, Grandma's large vanity, a few larger pieces to drive to the city dump. In the attic, we found Grandma's beautiful silk-and-fur dressing gown, with a wedding note from her future mother-in-law. The family into which she had married was, by all accounts, generous. Katie had held the delicate fabric in the tips of her fingers and smiled. The coloring had yellowed with age. Along the seams there were holes where insects had eaten their way to the other side. All the wedding presents were still in the original boxes. When Katie had asked Grandma about them, later, at dinner at the home, her eyes had lit up. The store was the best in town, she said; the gifts had all been so nice. She hadn't wanted to ruin any of them by wearing them.

At the end of our long moving day, Katie and I went for coffee at the franchise shop on State Highway. It was a weeknight, not too busy. The smell of roasting coffee and the high-gloss jazz were ritualized and generic; we might arrive at that exact moment mid-song to any franchise in the country. But we were beat after the move and homesick to be anywhere else, so I sat with the newspaper while Katie got to chatting with a woman sitting alone at the next table. Her daughter, the woman said, was visiting for the holidays. Her son had just left. She was out doing some shopping for dinner and needed a pick-me-up. I didn't quite follow the conversation, but I watched Katie's face for that familiar sequence of frowns and nods, her matter-of-fact tone, her careful listening. Katie had reverted into sounding-board mode. They were working out a problem together. To me, the woman was lonely in a way that made me nervous. I thought that any chat might become still more exhaustion after our exhausting day. Katie listened and smiled and asked questions. I put the paper down and turned my chair, though by then the chat was pleasant and general. Perhaps my joining made it less intimate. Or Katie had steered the conversation, as she usually did, toward easy rapport. As the woman left, she wished us a Merry Christmas. She smiled at Katie and thanked for her listening.

Why didn't I remember *that* Katie more often? The question troubled me with its suggestion of certainty. Was I only remembering one Katie now, a Katie whom I had married young, and now happily set on the pyre and pushed into open waters, offering my eager sacrifice to unhappiness, that she had died and I would live as though I was supposed to love someone else? I had said all year that I would not make Katie into a martyr or a saint, that I would remember *all* of Katie and honor that memory by telling the truth. Had I told too much of it? Did I remember the bad in order to live well after the good?

The day after Grandma's funeral, we said our good-byes over breakfast at the hotel. I left first thing and drove north all day to Sioux Falls, then west across South Dakota to the Badlands. Even without a reservation, a last-minute cancellation meant I could spend two nights still in the national park and the next night at a motel near its entrance. The morning after that, I would meet Cait in Billings.

*

*Badlands.* In translation, *the hard place to cross, the wasted land, the empty valleys inside black hills.* Fossil hunters still went there to find imaginary sea creatures. Homesteaders lost their farms to locust plagues and frosts and the Dust Bowl. I was there for Theodore Roosevelt. I had read all summer about his self-imposed exile in the Badlands after the death of his first wife, Alice. How he had set out to make a second life, to grieve and revive a different past, one from which he might become instead the naturalist Rough Rider, the industrial ornithologist—a life to which the past could not, in the end, cling. He wrote it this way in his journal: "The light in my life has gone out." He wrote nothing else about it. He refused to say or write Alice's name ever again, even to their daughter, her namesake, though friends noticed how he worried during his second wife Edith's five pregnancies, so different were his moods then from the usual ebullient and willful happiness.

Hadn't widowhood suggested clear rituals for doing things carefully and right in order to see a grief finished? In the storage locker across town, I had broken down the last boxes of our life. I had given away Katie's shirts, jewelry, books, posters, and cowboy boots, even her bowling ball. We had planted wildflowers near her ashes. And yet, a corresponding peace of mind was never entirely forthcoming. It lingered in the near distance, shrouded in a haze I kept thinking would lift, which time did not clear. The feeling was of having skipped important steps, but also of working too quickly toward an end, of trying and failing to be done with grief. Real widowers, I told myself, wheeled the samsara of grief indefinitely, perpetually bereft, unsteady in the living—the loving—world. A feeling of cutting away the past seemed nearly equal to my ambition to cross the Badlands, where I was sure such ambivalences would end, if only that a next life, as fragile and susceptible to chance as the life before it, might finally begin.

The Badlands rose from the west in near miniature, no bigger than my thumb. Black Hills staggered them into columns and fists, a horizon of discarded pipes stuck in the Earth, welded at the tips and set out to gather heat and dry the land. Few told this origin story, except to say the formation of the outcrops had been beautiful and strange—in spite of such seeming barrenness, quite full of life. Here was the place I had meant for months to spend my last days alone before setting out for California; a beginning that would make no circle to any other part of my life. Roosevelt had come west, off and on, for years, but in my mind, it was a single sequence. The place was so spectacular he needed only to go there once.

My room just off the ranger station was small, with no electricity. I laid out my clothes, locked the car, and set off on a seventeen-mile bike ride that a ranger had recommended, into the nearby reservation, along the highway, and back through the entrance. I was alone most of the way. There were signs for rattlesnakes, bobcats, rams, and bison, but all I ever heard in that Martian landscape, shrinking at night into miniature relief, was the soggy clump of weeds and gravel under my tires. Back in my room, the disappearing light turned the walls gray, then red. The next morning, I unstrapped the bike, clipped the front wheel into position, filled the plastic bladder with water, and set out on the same loop. Even halfway across the country, in this uncertain place, I liked my circles. The last morning, I rode a mile before I noticed the air was low. I couldn't find the leak. I walked back into the park, hooked the bike onto the car again, and drove to the nearby town. All that jostling on the highway, the taking down and tying up, and the riding across trails, meant the bike was bending, slightly, along the frame. It needed half its parts repaired, a few others replaced. The bike shop owner explained that he could keep it running for another month or so but I should probably buy a new bike when I got to California. In the meantime, there was blasting happening most afternoons at the Crazy Horse Memorial. I might take a lunch into the foothills, head over to see the four presidents, then come back around closing time.

Returning to the park, I again paid the ranger ten dollars. I powered down my cell phone, unloaded my pack and bike, and walked the winding mile between miniature canyons, a perfect facsimile of mountains, maybe sixty feet tall, with a road through the shallowest parts, and bluffs that dropped into vast, colorless valleys. Down the path, the peaks looked taller. The sky itself was brilliant and blue. A wooden placard at the entrance to the trail gave helpful hints for how to avoid opportunistic predators. Clap one's hands and grunt to startle coyotes. Walk in pairs and never leave the trail. However I turned with the trail, I found still another delicate and unmarked offshoot, a path only a few hundred yards from a scenic overview or nature station where strangers stood together with maps and field guides and cameras. Following such trails, I did not feel triumphant. I tried to imagine that the walking itself was a ritual, but I didn't really believe it. I arrived at my small cabin and found again the empty room with a cot, a sink, and a low table with a simple lamp. I packed my bag and walked out to the car.

That last night, I moved into the motel just past the park entrance. The motel sign made the only brightness for miles. There were outcrops in the darkness, but my eye drifted to the horizon and up. I hadn't seen so many stars in the sky since the night Katie had died. The mountain sky, at elevation, had seemed so close to the ground. At the edge of the parking lot, I looked for the constellations I recognized. When that didn't work, I named all of the ones I didn't, if only that, from indistinct patterns and swaths of light, some suggestion of order might fall across and over me. I had taken on good faith that the Badlands were bear-less, so I stood a while longer looking up, enjoying the quiet of the desert until it got too cold, and then I doubled back, trying not to look directly at the sign. When I did, I nearly went blind. When I didn't, I couldn't see my way. Near the vending machines, an Indian doctor traveling from Siberia to Las Vegas was smoking cigarettes and waiting for a pizza. He would head back in a few weeks to start his residency in a remote part of Russia. How many more places would he go that summer, in no particular direction, until it was simply time to leave? I understood that kind of traveling: always lost, but never really lost. Occupied by an absence of purpose, however temporary. But I couldn't say that, and since I knew nothing about Russia, and very little about India, our conversation petered out. I said goodnight and unlocked the door to my room. I flipped through the cable movies, set a wake-up call, and fell asleep thinking about Cait. The rocks in the morning were epic and tiny. It took less than an hour to drive the rest of the way through the park.

\*

The Billings, Montana, airport was little more than a stopover, a short building fenced a few miles in every direction, with a tower and radio, double-glass doors, and private airplanes crammed to one side of the field. I pulled my car right up to the gate. *No wonder,* I thought, *Cait had to take three planes to get here.* Heads of dead animals decorated the baggage claim. The usual candy and soda were for sale in the gift shop, beside sunglasses and paperbacks and a few local wares that looked homey and worn on the shelf. The flowers, at least, were reasonably fresh.

*I am supposed to be here,* I told myself. *I got myself to Billings so that this moment would happen.* Sally Todd's fainting sofa and William Howard Taft's enormous claw-footed bathtub waited together, in replica, at the entrance to the presidential-themed bed-and-breakfast I had booked online. Past the runways, I could see mountains in every direction and the small bowl of a valley scrubbed into the land centuries earlier, where two cities seemed now to float across a high lake.

It was so beautiful, this West, so unfairly beautiful. Even the throwaway places brimmed with promise and hope and life. I thought of

Grandma's question. *What do they take us for, anyway?* Every impulse to discovery seemed rewarded here. A whole history of failures, person to person, magnified by so much ambition to peak, cross, circle, sound, mine, and plot, hardly registered in these bright rivers with high cliffs and miles upon miles of open space. I watched the monitor for Cait's arrival. I ran the numbers in my mind, taking the difference of the bike repair, gas money, food, motel, and lodge charges, against what I had left in the bank.

What was I going to buy that we wouldn't find together?

Who was ever ready for a next life to begin?

I caught in the reflection of the sunglasses on the rotating shelf my enormous and circumspect face, beaming, seemingly so happily trusting and naïve, so optimistic, with my stocky build and my habit of leaning down to talk to people so I didn't seem too tall or intimidating. What didn't he know that I was about to discover? He didn't know anything about me or what I wanted. He knew everything about me, especially what I wanted. Katie had known it, too, even before she had married me. How little I was sometimes capable of. How easily I was overwhelmed. What I feared and resented in the people I loved, and especially, what I was willing to take for granted. She knew all those evenings I had wasted, pacing back and forth in our apartment in Uptown, insisting we marry, and wondering if I had any talent to do the things I really loved. Once, to end a fight, I had blurted out the secret of the book we were reading for book club. *Piggy DIES!* I had loved my victory in the moment. I had felt terrible about it for weeks. *Look at you,* Katie's look seemed to say. *What a victory.* How many of those moments would ever really go forgotten in a second life? What worse things would Cait know that Katie never did?

Already, people were walking out from the gate. My hands were cold. Beneath the deer carcass, beside a shelf of freshly tapped Montana maple syrup, I would see Cait and hold her, and know, once and for all, what was real. I had only to say it. Yes, it's been long enough. I have put myself through the middle space in as many ways as I can imagine. I have lingered there, double- and triple-checking myself for wellness, sanity, trauma, and precedent, and now it is time to continue. The other side waits to take away everything in an instant. So what. I still want this. I want this more than anything else, and I will do this better. I will be a better man. More than the reassuring comforts of misery and diminishment, I want to see Cait and love her. I want to love the West and to find there some variation on what everyone agrees is happiness, a variation on me. I will never again be that man who watched Katie die and was unable to stop it. I will always be that man, and I might even learn to like him. And if I see him watching me, waiting for me to fail, with such knowing smugness from every mirrored square on a sunglass rack, then we will wait together. One of us is right. And it was in such careful worrying about what was going to happen next that I missed her anyway, I who had come all this way for the simple purpose of finding her had nearly lost both of us in a sunglass rack. Cait walked out from security, from the end of a vast wall of trophied animals, walked and smiled, so happy to see me, impressed by the droopy flowers in my arms, and certain, as nothing else in a life, that I was there for *her*. I had come all this way *just for her*. She was here, now, and she had found me. More than anything, she wanted this too.

# Crossing to Safety

## I.

The past is past: aggressive, ursine. I try not to poke at it. Katie is dead nine years. Our life, in memory, is loved too little. I should end our story there. I never do.

If Katie was alive, I know, I wouldn't think to envy this life. Walt's silky mop, once peach fuzz, would look as coarse and unfamiliar as any boy's hair. I might pause a moment to admire his inelegant tromp, the compulsive fireman getup shading dinosaurs and finally *Star Wars*, his wandering across some grocery aisle or parking lot, into a car, a city, a different life that belongs to someone else, some other harried and aging man who can hardly keep up with the lisping boy who no longer toddles. It would mean nothing to cross each other's lives like that. This is what I know about my life after Katie's life: it makes a sequence I confuse constantly for order. Katie died and then I remarried. I was married to Katie and now I am married to

Cait. "Time is linear," someone says, to be helpful, the way someone used to say, "Katie cannot die again." At first, it was enough to love this second life after the first, perhaps even in spite of it; to see, in the absence of scale, an inevitable sequence, as though sequences do not make their own music, in phrases and patterns that repeat as a life continues. But if such distinctions begin a love story, our fable, my tale of *what comes next and how to like it*, then I know that the present is ursine too: persistent, enormous, accustomed to ritual, and easily indifferent.

Standing mid-river, I see no bears.

Which is not to say they are not there.

*

There are certain coincidences, synchronicities I notice but can't explain. A year to the day of Katie's death, the *New Yorker* runs a grizzly themed cover for the first time in thirty years. Brown bears leave the woods wearing the backpacks and cellphones of hikers. *No Picnicking in Buffalo Wilds.* Two months later, the highway out of Montana takes Cait and me across Beartooth Pass, up and down Beartooth Highway. There are bear totems in the shops of the cities on either side of the pass and a museum with mounted brown bears, arms splayed and teeth bared. An uncle at Cait's family cabin pins photos of a black bear sitting on the porch earlier that week. We arrive the next day. On our wedding day, as Cait walks down the aisle, it starts to rain. It hasn't rained in her city on that day for decades. The rain stops as soon as the ceremony begins. The editor of my book about Katie is named Katy. The agent I work with is named Katherine. For two years, I share an office with a colleague whose sister-in-law, Kathryn, was a Peace Corps volunteer who worked in public health and died a year before Katie died. On a family trip to Colorado, I come back from dinner to find bear scat on the porch of our rented house. My brother takes photographs. Hiking a trail the next day, he follows a bear with its cubs to a river. Among seventeen hundred new students at the university where I teach, the valedictorian from

Katie's high school is randomly assigned to my six-student group of advisees. He is the first student from her high school to ever attend the university. He remembers Katie's wake and the all-day traffic. Cat Stevens's "Peace Train" is the song I hear on rooftops and in bars across Chicago all summer when I visit on the first anniversary of Katie's death. Katie loved Cat Stevens. "Peace Train" is the song that plays on the radio as we drive to the hospital where Cait gives birth to our first son, Walt. The due date for our second son, Sam, is the fifth anniversary of Katie's death. We induce four days early to avoid the coincidence. Our healthy baby boy is born with blue eyes and a mop of dark hair that lightens to red, like mine, in the summer sun. At a party the next month, a man who knows my father-in-law corners me to show the little moons of scar tissue on his throat. He brags his showdown with a bear near Lake Tahoe, his triumph at fending it off. My bear, I think to myself, would kill your bear. *My bear was ten times as big as yours,* I want to say, *and it killed my fucking wife.* But he doesn't know about Katie, and I don't want to embarrass my father-in-law, much less begin in anger a critique I can hardly make heads or tails of myself. It is the stranger's story to tell. He enjoys telling it. The bear is the mechanism of his persuasion: what he once survived that someone else should now believe. Surely, I can sympathize. I smile politely and ask questions. I excuse myself, and a little later, across the room, I watch him tell the story, word for word, to someone else. Three years later, near Lake Tahoe, Cait and I cross the path of a black bear and its cubs. I hold two rocks in my hands and wait for them to pass. They are garbage bears: not predators. They pass down the river, toward other, more remote cabins. Or so I tell myself. The next week, Cait's sister posts a photo of a black bear on the beach of the large lake near the cabin. Walt is standing beside her as she takes the photograph. Sam is in the water. The baby is asleep inside the cabin. The bear is running down the beach, slightly out of focus, through a family picnic. Everyone at the picnic is photographing it.

*

Nearly every zoo in America I visit has a bear. A few have several. Only the largest have brown bears. Whenever we push our boys in the stroller past the penguins and otters, toward the spiders and chinchillas, Cait and I invariably end up a few right turns away. Some habitat—a pen, really, a crude enclosure—makes the daily life of a bear transparent to our curiosity. The bears come and go. At a distance, without intrusion, they sleep on long slabs of cement, wrestle each other, and disappear into habitats. Between meals, they make circles around the inner glass. They neither hunt nor roam. Their boredom is epic and unforgiving. Absurd, nihilistic, and terrifyingly literal, such bears are, finally, everything except a *bear*.

"Of the strength and ferocity of this animal the Indians had given us dreadful accounts," wrote Meriwether Lewis in his journal on April 29, 1805. "He rather attacks than avoids a man, and such is the terror which he has inspired, that the Indians who go in quest of him paint themselves and perform all the superstitious rites customary when they make war on a neighboring nation." A half century later their outsized legend was finished. Men prospected, then died to tell it. The stories moved east as fast as silver. The land was picked clean of grizzlies and turned inside out. Wrapped as pelts, their heads mounted on clapboard walls, the brown bear became, in ornament, extinct and ubiquitous. The tributes were nearly kitsch: statues, rugs, coatracks, coins, mats, university mascots, even the state seal. Where the last grizzlies disappeared from the Sierras, the scrubbier black bear survived in their place—*survive*—to scamper unseen down trails and across the porches of cabins in spring, no bigger than a large dog. Even from a distance, the resemblance is minor. Claws are short where they should lengthen. Shoulders round rather than hump. Soaked in chemicals and set out to withstand the seasons, the totem preens, while the pest disappears all winter into colorful anecdotes—cub in blueberries, mama on the slopes—by which the witness brags his savvy. In miniature, a history is brought full circle. We are tolerant.

"The sow was fierce and mighty," Lewis wrote, "but I knew to stand still until she passed."

\*

Every summer, we make our crossing. We take our boys to a cabin on the far side of a lake that John Muir called "the most delightful place in all the famous Tahoe region. From no other valley, as far as I know, may excursions be made in a single day to so many peaks, wild gardens, glacier lakes, glacier meadows, and alpine groves, cascades and the like." There, at the edge of Desolation Wilderness, we unlock doors and cupboards, open windows, roll out mattresses, carry in groceries and supplies. Cait and her mom row back and forth from the parking lot to the dock while I hike the long way around on the path. There are boulders near the lake where the path turns from the trees. There is running water from a higher stream to the cabin, but no plumbing. The cabin is wired for electricity, with a wood stove to warm the loft at night. Other cabins stagger along the hill, up and down the mountain, nine in all spaced a few hundred yards apart, on a path between them that does not reach the other side of the lake. From the porch I can see the peak of one roof and, father below, the boathouse. We are not quite remote and not entirely close to anywhere. The year that marmots eat through the wiring of our car, it takes all day to run a tow truck up the hill.

It takes maybe twenty minutes to walk the long way around from the cabin to the parking lot. The water is cold and high for the season. Trees converge in all directions to a single point of shade surrounded by light. I know this hike to where the little bridge is washed out. No big deal. It is the custom on the hill to make a new bridge each spring. Cabin owners damn the water with sticks and rocks to slow the erosion, as the beavers do each spring, raising the lake. In a few hours, I know, Cait will walk around and fix it, or her brother-in-law, the economist, will come later in the week to jerry-rig a separate path. I try one way across, careful, then double back. I hike a little ways up the river to see if there is a better path. How have I gotten lost in such a narrow space? There is another path that winds up the mountain. The ground is softer higher on the hill. I can't quite make out the place where the trail starts back. I don't trust my footing in the water. *What am I doing,* I think, *in the woods by myself?* I am breathing at high altitude, a little faster than I mean to, in the exaggerated manner of a person trying too hard to relax. But the trail is nearby. I know it. I can see it in my mind, past the bridge, and maybe a few hundred yards away, on the lake in the blue and red rowboat, Cait. I listen for the oars on the water. That scent on the air—no, the taste in my mouth: bitter, metallic. I cannot stop reassuring myself. *This is normal too,* I think, though what follows is less helpful: *It begins like this too.*

I let the white earbuds fall to my side and close my eyes. I listen for any noise I might recognize: a far cry for help, an approaching grunt. *No one is going to die* is too silly and vivid—too much. I am standing by a lake in the woods in California. Someone is crying for help. I can hear the pitch of a voice over the noise of the water. No, that's my phone. A tinny radio podcast ticks and hisses at my hip. I have forgotten to stop it. Anyone nearby would hear it. Anything. Something is watching me. Nonsense. *These aren't even the right bears,* I remind myself. As certain and impractical as reason itself: *There are bears in these woods, and you are far from the trail.*

There are rumors that the Forest Service has for years relocated brown and black bears from Yellowstone into Desolation Wilderness, though people mostly see the black bears. Black bears knock down half the cabin doors every winter, tear open the fridges and pantries, and shit on the living room rugs. Every season, someone comes to repair the bridges, and someone else rehinges the doors, and someone drives all the way to Raleigh's in South Lake Tahoe to buy gin and tonic water so that everyone can get drunk quickly at altitude. No one worries about black bears. They are not predators. Hungry and foraging, moving farther from the cities into narrower tracts of high desert plain, black bears keep wide and far of the snowshoeing locals who make a sport of opening cabins for the holidays. Come summer, especially during a drought, the bears leave the high streams and rivers to amble through the parking lots, into the outhouses and beyond the lake where, at dusk, someone is often photographing a cub as it bathes itself, insisting the sighting is good luck and posting the picture on social media.

I watch the trees, which are not moving. I can hear the water moving. What is the point of all that therapy, the weekly call I keep even when we visit the cabin, those Friday mornings I drive into town, park at the supermarket, and sit with my engine running for exactly one hour, charging my cell phone and scribbling notes about trauma and integrity on the backs of envelopes, car service statements, and candy wrappers—any paper I can find in the car—if I do not, in such a moment, start walking? And if I walk in circles, doubling back an hour later along the trail, following on foot the long way across the hill and around the lake and finally find Cait near the parking lot, where she ferries me across and says, "It's a lovely day. We can see all the way to the far peaks"; if she names the peaks should I agree, "Yes, they are beautiful"? If I survive another year at the cabin, will the next year feel less strange and terrifying? Will my boys, here, become sensible and rugged in nature, scraping knees and bruising themselves day after day, so happy in the mountains, where the blood makes terrific goose eggs on their foreheads, as I make myself lonely with each failed prognostication at every dark shape that never fumbles out of trees? Because no one else really shares my fear of this place. Surely what they find most compelling, if less and less interesting, is that most obvious fact of my life, the one I have lived all of this time with the hope of simply living after. *Poor John*, I imagine they will say, *he didn't come up this year. You know he lost his first wife in woods just like these.*

## 2.

*I was happy. I didn't keep a journal. I rested my head on your shoulder, and you kept driving west. How far since Billings? How much farther to Utah? We passed mountains, canyons, and sulfur pools. We passed buffalo, mountain goats, and squirrels. In the Gardner River swimming hole a Korean couple happily scalded their white skin. Clouds clung to the outcrops. You named widgeons, stills, and rails. You named sisters, cousins, and aunts. I said that when your boyfriend left the city that winter to attend a Rambo premiere in Las Vegas, it gave me hope. How from Dolores Park a few months later this generous city lit everything: streetcars and pylons, porch lamps and ships, the Bay Bridge but not the Golden Gate. We ate ribs, chicken, and brisket. We drove US-212, State Road 3, I-90. Crossing the Beartooth Pass, the glacial air was thin and cold mist rose on the water. A petrified spruce felled by lightning peaked the tree line at dusk. We left Wyoming to enter Yellowstone. We left the lodge to walk to our cabin. I don't know how the heart makes decisions. Maybe love is something born again in different bodies so it can keep moving forward. On the wall of a diner, just past Heart Lake, the rangers nailed simple, hand-painted warnings. We saw nothing until suddenly, everywhere, the sound of antlers, like ice chipped from a roof. It made no sense to count them.*

*

We drove Highway 212 out of Billings and across the Little Bighorn River. The turnoff was a small road from the highway that went straight up the hill to a parking lot. Three or four souvenir shops sold all manner of headdresses, plastic revolvers, playing cards, and feathers. Buffalo and vista postcards were three for a dollar. Next to a photo of Dustin Hoffman, a shoebox took donations for the local arts center. There were snakes in the grass that time of year, and handmade markers on sticks numbering various stages of the famous battle, showing the movements of Union, Sioux, and Cheyenne soldiers on the hill. We were encouraged to check their movements against our souvenir map. In one patch of brown grass, a few men on horses had turned the whole war. The next summer, they camped across the Dakotas one last time as free people. The exhibits in the museum seemed mostly to argue about the legacy of Custer. He was a coward, a hero, the little general, the stone face of no surrender, a patsy of bureaucratic big government, yet another bearded face of white oppression. No one, it seemed, really knew Custer all that well or understood why he was

so keen to capture women and children. Nor did they know whether
Crazy Horse had surrounded Custer and pressed to the center or
made instead one great charge up and over the top, slaughtering the
horses and scattering the terrified soldiers. On the other side of Last
Stand Hill, white and black crosses marked the death sites of soldiers.
We walked a narrow and circling path to reach the very top. Other
tourists parked at the lookout and crossed the main road. Down the
trail, a ranger said to rustle the grass as we approached the ravine. We
wouldn't see the rattlesnakes, he said, but we might hear them coming.

"What noise," I asked, "does a rattlesnake make?"

"Well, he usually rustles the grasses at your feet."

What a strange place, we agreed, for a first date. Cait had flown all
the way to Montana to meet me for my drive west, and I had taken
her here. I said that it was too bad the summer hills were covered in
dead grass.

Cait laughed.

"The grass isn't dead," she said. "It just turns that color in summer."

I shuffled my feet against the gravel to make as much noise as possible. She laughed at that too. At the far edge of the map, the ranger
pointed out a hospital to which tourists raced every few weeks, a belt
wrapped just above the wound site, the heartiest among them sucking
valiantly to slow the circulation of venom. The hospital was stocked
with antivenom. A nurse measured a syringe and made a note on the
computer. The hospital was in Billings, our city for the night. Our
beautiful and temporary bed and breakfast had five rooms named for
five different presidents and an owner who, seeing my bumper sticker,
wouldn't stop making Obama jokes. Why can't Barack Obama dance?
Because he has two left-ist feet! As the crow flies, it would be, what,
three or four miles to the hospital? But we had time. Our strange date
was memorable. We would always remember it: the sandwiches at the
airport, the invisible and ubiquitous snakes, the markers and crosses
stuck in the hill. Where else could the courtship go but up? Even
the dead-looking spots teemed with possibility: great rolling plains
buckling across the valley, with no shelter from the sun and no place

to hide except in the lowest parts, those small patches of shade where lavender bushes and wild sage went soft at night and the snakes hid from the day's heat on the cool pavement under cars.

*

At the bed and breakfast, we unpacked our bags into a lacquered dresser with clawed feet. We took showers, changed our clothes, and sat on the bed, reading old magazines someone had left on the side table. *People do this all the time*, I told myself, meaning sometimes old friends sit together on a bed reading magazines in the early afternoon, and other times, new lovers rip off each other's clothes and wear the bed right through the ceiling of the kitchen. In the reflection of the old-fashioned vanity, I could see the whole room. Cait was reading *Newsweek* and *People*. I should take as my cue, I thought, the faces of the small children struggling with the stigma of so much bad nutrition and wheezing. *Childhood Obesity: The Silent Epidemic*. Did their ardent and curious faces kill the mood? Should I sweep Cait into my arms and smell the shampoo on her skin?

And if we kissed like that, would it feel good—*if there was chemistry*—to enjoy this last first part of falling in love? The possibility ran like a bolt down the back of my neck. It made my fingers warm. On the opposite page: fat kids, fireworks. A space rocket launched across a pill ad. A woman perched in a grandfather clock cheered wildly the arrival of her bottle of perfume. *And is it really worth it?* I thought. *Is now the right time?* As though I might forget how suddenly the body notices itself when it refuses to make a decision; the heavy heartbeat pinned under the ears, the limbs sunk in cement and refusing to lift. Yes, this was one moment. And if nothing happened, there would be other moments, right? We had the week ahead of us. We talked about it all summer. If not this week, then in California; if not this year, then next year. And yet, the Taft bedroom was ours for the night. It was mostly bed, a conversation piece for sure, billed as goods, the high palace of Taftian obesity and somnambulism, so spacious, I thought, that we'd at the very least get a good night's sleep. So I said to Cait—

"I think you should put that magazine down and kiss me now"
—and she did, and yes, that *was* the first moment, who knew?
And I liked it, it was *full of chemistry*; so we kissed a while on the bed,
rolling back and forth across ol' Taft. We got dressed and walked into
Billings, Montana, The Magic City, where a giant theater marquee
flashed the names of touring bands. We drank champagne and ate
french fries, ordered drinks, and split some chocolate thing stuffed
with chocolate and in a cake shape. And when Cait pulled me under
the street lamp, kissed me, and looked me dead in the eyes—
    "I think we should wait a little while before we take this thing all
the way"
—I thought exactly what I said. "I'm fine with that. That sounds
great."

*

All week, I drove. Cait told family stories. A high-end cruise line that
opened on Black Monday had sunk the family fortune. Her father
jumped out of helicopters and chased snakes and tree frogs across the
African continent. A cousin who probably wasn't a spy worked for
the organization that everyone agreed didn't secretly run the world.
Right away, I set a soundtrack of upbeat, sunny songs: early Dolly
Parton, late My Morning Jacket, James Taylor's *Greatest Hits*. The
music was simple and happy. Corny. One night, crossing Salt Lake
City, I played all my country-and-western tunes, as fast as I could
queue them. Katie's favorites were the back half of the catalogue. It
felt irreverent and weirdly sincere to hear them now, as though some
part of two affections could interconnect over the radio so long as
I didn't think too hard about the overlap. Cait loved the patriotic
ones. "My god," she asked, as I told her about karaoke in Indiana
on the Fourth of July, when all the sad men kept singing "Beer for
My Horses," "do such people really exist?" *They don't,* I thought, *live
in California.* I played the song a few times in a row. It became our
anthem. We arrived each day a little farther west: Montana, Idaho,
Utah, Nevada. We drove like that for hours at a time, telling stories,

listening to songs and podcasts, tuning in to whatever news we could find in the mountains.

How far could I lean across the car toward Cait? How long could I hold that pose and keep the road more or less in front of us, with the sun in our eyes and the gas gauge ticking ever closer to empty? I never wanted to leave the car, not for any reason. I didn't want anything to disrupt our easy happiness. In the woods, on a day hike, Cait asked again, was I worried about bears? Were the mountains okay? I was doing fine, I told her; it would all be fine. The Rockies were so much larger than the Carpathians. I had read online that brown bears lived farther north, in Canada and Alaska. It was mostly true. No one had killed a brown bear in the wild for nearly a century, though the populations were tracked year to year. A brown bear hadn't killed a tourist away from a zoo all summer, as far as anyone could tell.

Driving into Yellowstone, we got stuck in a herd of buffalo. Cars were stopped eight and nine deep, with all the drivers leaning out to take pictures. I felt so safe, I said, inside our car. I think I meant it. Buffalo weren't bears. They seemed indifferent to us, passing beside our windows and between our bumpers, easy and slow and deliberate, as though they did this all the time. Probably, they did. Their hair smelled like wet wool. They grunted and butted each other as they moved. Certainly, it would take only a few nudges to roll our car across the highway and into the ditch. It would be a free-for-all there. But I didn't know how buffalos spooked. I wasn't sure, even, what they ate. I assumed they were friendly and meant well. I tried to enjoy the buffalo. Everyone was taking pictures.

The road opened up again. It was getting dark. We had planned to drive across the park and stay in one of the cities just past the exit, but we had hardly gone a quarter of the way. Now, the roads were empty. It was the last week of the season. We stopped at the Roosevelt Lodge and asked if they had any rooms to rent. No one had arrived to claim the last cabin, the clerk said. It was ours if we wanted it. We ate dinner on the wraparound porch and then sat out on oversized rocking chairs, watching the stars. Someone had made a fire. As it chattered and snapped at the cold night, we huddled close. There were signs on the stairs, and again between the cabins, warning what to do if we saw a grizzly, how the bear was likely to react, the few and simple things we might have brought with us on our hike or purchased from the lobby store that could buy us precious seconds to flee, distract, disinterest, survive. From the porch, it was a lovely view of the sky. In the middle of the woods, miles from any light pollution, there seemed no end in any direction. Cait named minor constellations. I made up the names of a few—Rastraya the Dancer, Septum Minor—but she caught on. Then, we talked about ourselves. It was beautiful to feel so in love, as though the great negotiation we had begun months earlier was now stuck up in the stars, and we could simply admire it, falling all around us in its certainty. Leaning into the light, Cait was there. I knew what we were thinking. I liked that certainty. It made me feel powerful and bright. Back at the cabin, I locked the door, pulled Cait close, and slept straight through the night.

*

Up the Beartooth Pass, Cait said, "Let's stop for candy." Our last city before the climb was tourist friendly and flush. Official-looking squares of painted aluminum warned passersby, Grin & Bear It! and over the lumbering silhouette of a grizzly, Peak Show Ahead! From plastic bins we filled plastic bags with taffy and gummy worms. We spent the next hour digging pastel wax from wax paper, stretching the neon gelatin to twice its length, winding our way up the mountain, past the tree line. Cait leaned across the seat and closed her eyes. James Taylor was singing on the radio about Carolina on his mind. On the display over the dash, the temperature outside ticked down a few more degrees. The sky clouded over. The engine raced furiously to keep minimum speed on a stretch of interstate nearly empty of other cars. At each switchback, we could see all the way across the mountain. There were clearings in the trees there, and boulders rimmed with sand. Further up, the grass was gone. The paved roads were darker than the surrounding hills, but I could see them still, the wide roaming paths where no humans came and went at a distance. Were the high alpine lakes stocked with fish? Did deer stop there to drink? All I really wanted to feel was Cait's head on my shoulder, how beautifully the mountains, up close, trimmed the gray sky, and what had it been, at least twenty years since a grizzly had attacked and killed someone in Montana?

I wanted to prove something.

I had no idea what I was doing.

"Let's stop here," I said, "and walk around that lake."

At the turnout, the wind whipped open our doors. It was loud there, and colder still than either of us had expected. Cait dug sweatshirts out of our bags and two wool caps. She had grown up spending summers in country like this, surrounded by aunts and uncles, older siblings and cousins, who set out each morning into the wilderness with one happy rule: home before dusk. Past the turnout, there was a small trail between the trees. We were on the ridge now. In every direction, we could see level, open space and a horizon flat and gray as the sky overhead. Cait held my hand and pulled me up onto a rock. The water was right below us. The lake was no bigger than a swimming pool. In a few minutes, I thought, we could get back to the car. If I had my keys out, we could both push into the passenger seat and get the door closed in less than a minute. Why had I left my phone in the car? Surely, another car was coming this way. It would pass in a few minutes. I thought, *The noise of cars at this altitude, the flat land, the few places for cover in any direction, the few trees* and *Bears do not cross during the day* and *This place is filled to the fucking brim with bears, in every direction, around every corner and behind even these pitiful rocks that give us, what, six inches of high ground?*, which is when I knew I'd outplayed myself. I would have to ask for help. My bravado, my upping of the ante, a full-on machismo pissing into the wind, proved nothing. I was terrified. Cait was talking to me. She had been talking the whole time, and smiling, holding up sprigs for me to smell, snapping off tree leaves I could rub in my palm to bring out the scent, telling a story about her childhood that began with off-trail hiking and ended at waterfalls near glacial lakes with jumping rocks sixty or seventy feet off the ground. Someone died there every couple of years. All summer, tourists and locals made the delirious plunge, swam back to shore, and told the tale.

"Can you just," I said, trying to find the words. "I mean, would you—would it be okay—can you, you know, maybe hold me?"

So maybe she was thinking it too—what was on my mind that we had so quickly stopped—that I had stopped talking. She smiled and reached out her arms, pulling me in sideways. She filled in the silence with whatever came to mind, and even after a few moments, when I said I was okay, as we walked back to the car, she said there might be bears at this altitude, but probably not so close to a highway, not in the middle of the day. Bears near people learned their routines and kept a distance. They were shot when they didn't. And I wanted to agree with her and say also that they would be black bears instead of grizzlies, across the rest of the state, at least until we got to Yellowstone, that I was grateful for her reassurance because she knew these places well and I did not. But still, I wondered: Did snakes cross the tree line at altitude? Mountain lions? Cougars? Did hunters at this altitude wear orange vests? Should tourists? Did the rain bring thunder, lightning, fire? If a semi lost control on the downhill, what were the odds that the driver would make it to the runaway truck ramp before he rolled the tank across all four lanes, sparking the metal on the edge of the divider, clearing us off the edges of the map, into an echo of fire and dust?

*

We drove the last stretch all day to arrive at her family's cabin. Past Salt Lake City, we set out with the sun behind us until it crossed overhead and bore down against our progress. The desert was hot and bright. The last news we heard, leaving the city, was that John McCain had picked Sarah Palin as his running mate. "Who is Sarah Palin?" Cait asked. I knew all about Sarah Palin from my podcasts. Sarah Palin, I explained, was the governor of Alaska, a choice-friendly and modest centrist who worked well with big business and urban liberals and who had a reputation for being a small-town politico on the make. Such went the conventional wisdom, and our fears that drive, and for many days following, that McCain might turn the country bright red with his moderate genius.

Coming down the hill past Tahoe, the mountains gave way to terrific bends and plunges. West was our time to make up, our certain destination, and now, our deadline. Cait's family was gathering at the cabin for the holiday weekend. If we got there by sunset, we could have dinner and meet everyone. As we drove, Cait talked about her good friend who had married after her boyfriend made a terrific PowerPoint presentation. There were slides and graphs, bulleted arguments and calculations, expressed in complicated equations, by which he had meticulously predicted their future. Two to four kids. A home in the hills near Portland. Trips each summer to see her family and, if they were lucky, a trip every spring by themselves to the beachside timeshare he said they'd be nuts not to buy into. It was all hypothetical, but the numbers had a certain magic to them. He had worked out his arguments in advance. He reassured like a lawyer, finessing rougher points, bullying through easier ones, wearing her down until there was only one response. They married that fall, in the farmhouse he knew she'd like, with the guest list and seating chart he had anticipated within three seats of who actually showed up. Cait admired his determination and commitment, she said, even as there was something sterile about his method, a reckoning of sides of equations that meant things should equal out to perfect sums, with no remainders or carryovers and nothing left to chance. It wasn't *romantic*, Cait said. I oriented myself instantly to this assessment. Was I romantic? In all my caution about leaving Indiana and racing to California, and planning for the future, had I left enough to the heart?

Then, we were arrived. I pulled up slowly along what seemed, in the darkness, a stone drawbridge. The tires dug into the gravel, inching us forward. I pulled the emergency break and took out the electronic key. It was the end of our trip. We had arrived in good time. Outside the car, we would walk into a world of family I had only the faintest notion could be so epic. Aunts and cousins who were best friends. Grandparents who held court at the heads of long tables. An entire clan of family traveled every Labor Day to that cabin in order to watch Cait's father lead cardboard boat races at the dock of the nearby lake. Of course, there were cardboard boat races. The children were smiling and building their cardboard boats out back. Uncles watched with pursed lips, nodding their heads. There was a hierarchy to the gathering, a continuity that took everything in and said that all the pieces fit. For everything I knew of family, this was both corollary and radical opposite. Surely, people who loved everyone simultaneously could not possibly be related. I had no idea how to situate myself within such extremes. I wasn't sure that I needed to. It seemed that I would soon marry near the heart of something special where Cait was beloved, without condition, admired and kept dear. I would notice it in the way she organized our introductions, and the knowing looks that followed the fast once-overs. People who were too busy to care too much about arrivals made a general exception for Cait.

Opening the car door, I noticed first the pine trees and ravines in the surrounding darkness. A porch light cast down the trail a faint circle that showed the way and made shadows. We were only a few dozen yards out, but the distance seemed immense. The porch looked so exposed. Cait turned me in another direction. We weren't going that way, not yet. Her mother had left a note to say they would all be down the hill at the neighbor's cabin. Cait knew the way by heart. We cut across the rocks and over what seemed like a giant river, though the next day, I would see the pathetic stream and the high, flat rocks across it. On the cabin porch, her father was playing the saxophone with a quartet of close friends. As we walked up the stairs, the procession began. As though in a chorus line, family members peeled away to say hello, hug Cait, hug me, and ask questions. How had our trip gone? Had we just arrived? Was I really from Indiana? Someone handed us glasses of wine. Someone else passed plates of pasta with salad, bread, sausages, and garden vegetables.

So many of the details I remembered were right. The aunt who lived in Northern California frequently came over to the house. She drove a red car. We talked like that a while. She was impressed by my memory. It was only the next day, saying hello on the beach, that I realized I had never met this woman. Rather, that spring, I had talked with her sister, a different aunt, nearly a twin. It was a family resemblance impossible to miss in the evening light and swirl of voices, drinks, meals, and conversations. Even after we had stumbled back finally to the family cabin and climbed into the tiny double bed, before we woke up all night with altitude dreams and the sound of pine combs, in the wind, falling onto the roof, I had to ask and ask again for Cait to help with the distinctions. There were five aunts, in total, eleven cousins, fifty-odd nephews and nieces and uncles and extended others. All afternoon, I had continued the conversation with the aunt I met the night before. Neither of us missed a beat. Only the next afternoon did I finally run out some part of my luck.

"What," Cait's mom asked, as we sat on the beach, "does your mother think of those tattoos?"

I rubbed the skin over my shoulder.

"She hates them."

"Oh, good," she said, walking into the water to swim. "We'll have something in common."

*

We hiked to a sulfur spring near a swimming hole and had a picnic. We drove the next day to an alpine lake with a lemonade stand and jumping rocks. Every time I tried to name a tree, I guessed *redwood* and got it wrong. There weren't redwoods this high up at elevation, not near the water. A family friend took us on a boat trip around the lake. We stopped to swim where, for decades, a recluse had prowled the beach with a shotgun, threatening trespassers. He was dead now. His land was cleared and filled with campers. The last night, we sat on the sofas, listening to her nephews coming and going in the kitchen. On the wall were two framed newspaper clippings related to a great-uncle's business and an acrostic poem extolling the virtues of a grandmother's career in journalism. I had been playing the acrostic game in my mind, ironically I guess, a little absent-minded. Can't take my eyes off of you. Clearly, we were meant for each other. Could I compare you to a summer's day? C for Compassionate, Caring, Consistent, Clever, Curvaceous, Cute, Charismatic. Corinthians, Cauliflower, Carpentry, Cumulus, Chard. California. From the Ben Folds Five song I had been singing all morning: "I wanna be Cait! Cait! Cait!"

"When we get back to the city," Cait said, "this is going to be exclusive, right?"

"I'm not sure," I said, "that that's a very good idea," but I didn't really catch her. I was already laughing. I was laughing so hard that I couldn't stop laughing, not even when my stomach seized up and I finally caught my breath, the tears on my face streaming down, and Christ, it felt good. I must have looked so odd, and I couldn't even explain the joke, not in any way that I thought would make sense, but yes, exclusive was just fine. Exclusive worked for me.

\*

Our last morning, I made a cup of coffee, said good-bye to everyone, and climbed back into the tiny green car. The family cabin and the nearby lake rolled into highway, so much silent exhaust coasting downhill, the engine charging the battery all the way, the battery icon on the dashboard one bar greener, nearly to full. I watched the steady decline of the mountains becoming fast relief, and the heavy trucks, loaded with goods and chemicals, toys and compounds, wheeling no clutch, awkward and confident on the breakaways, buoyant and joyless as teenagers on dirt bikes. It was an illusion. In a mile or so, the highway would incline back up. The trucks would fall away into profile, staggered as evenly as the hash marks separating traffic. At that speed, a single wreck would careen any vehicle down the mountain right into what I imagined was a valley, with trees blocking the high Sierra busk of all-day sun baking the pine silt, where ancient docks jutted over deep glacial lakes. I tried to imagine the prehistoric block of ice inching its way between the mountains, rimmed at the peaks. The external temperature on the dash ticked up a degree or so every few minutes. There was a computer somewhere in the car running calculations, firing one semiconductor alongside the next, spitting out a new set of data that made my progress into a kind of video game. Every five minutes, a yellow bar appeared on a timeline, measuring the efficiency of my driving habits. The far relief of one set of mountains and the near, jagged profile of the next meant, eventually, Central Valley. No romantic backdrop that. The highway was packed. The AC kicked in. The fruit crops in harvest sold at two and three dollars a pound.

Crossing Sacramento, I called my friend Dave in Chicago. He picked up on the first ring. He was so happy for me. Cait sounded wonderful. The trip must have been amazing. He had good news too. Meghan was thirteen weeks pregnant. She felt great, a little tired still. They were looking for a bigger place. *I can do this,* I thought to myself. *I can talk about someone else's happiness too.* There was enough happiness to go around. Out my window, the coastal hills of California were alive with matted, yellow grass. Between giant white windmills catching the ocean as it skipped over the hills, I pointed my tiny car at the end of a peninsula, through millions of invisible waves carrying my voice into the middle of the country. The waves found Dave's voice and carried it back with news of a life continuing, a new life in the instant that everything was changing, filling my world with infinite hopefulness, whichever parts bounced off the windshield or burned right through me, changing me as memory changes one life and connects it to the next, sometimes imagining the connections, renewing itself in order to find a way through.

## 3.

The bear followed me back across the lake. It swam beside us in the rowboat, climbed onto the roof of the cabin, and swatted at the trees until pinecones shook loose in twos and threes all night. It pissed under our window so that the whole room smelled of bear, and when I went out with the flashlight to say *aha!*, it disappeared just far enough back into the woods that I could see only the branches shaking with fear, and the pine needles scattering in both directions on the ground, and over my little beam of light, the sky filling in again with stars. There was no bear near the stream, and few bears anywhere close to the cabins. That time of year, in that part of the woods, they tended to get shot by the forest service, tagged by the fire patrol, or snapped into traps set on both sides of the lake. I could only panic there precisely because I *knew* I was safe. Only there, in my imagination, was the bear not quite afield. Only then could it stride forth to reveal itself, *wet-furred, in foot-by-foot-wide prints,* full and lumbering, graceful on its striped ball, squeezed into its tiny car just long enough to circle the circus, wave at the crowd, and then drive out of the tent and back deep into my subconscious.

For a while, this is how I thought about bears. The herd for an eye. A species for Katie. Destroy the world around them and see where they go next.

I see, in my rigid distinctions of species and place—brown and black, dead and alive, young widower and young dad, new husband and second wife—the suggestion of habit, an ending that brings me around again to what I only tell myself is a new beginning. But there is hopefulness, too, in such distinctions. I can't help looking for Katie where I do not miss her. It is easier, perhaps, than finding her where I am scared again to look.

I, too, lumber toward a beginning. From a remote and dark place, I come back every summer to the cabin so that I might revive the feeling, add another step to the ritual, and somehow, continue the rite. I want to say that nine months—one for each death anniversary—are missing from my life, but that isn't right. The time is there. I have lived through it. Every June, I hear my voice run out like a wire, charged and careless, eager to make a connection that closes the loop and returns me to this world. It is my voice, and my circling back and forth; my routine and my habit that I think might draw out all manner of calamity to begin the reckoning. I practice each to perfection. Once, I could imagine no life after Katie, much less one that meant me well; a life that leaves me now to see what I might do with so much fear and happiness.

From two ridges a surrounding life gathers near the cabin. Between them runs a river, high in the spring season, come down the mountain from the last snowpack, making a thin stream that always, eventually, runs dry. I have walked with Cait and our boys to the riverbank and back. Along the bed are stones set loose, rolling constantly this way and that. They make the path. Their edges are smooth. Their undersides, in the cold mud, are dry. The summer peaks round, in that high weather, to ice. Without ice, the river would hedge the land and stop its progress. The cabins would shutter. No one would return.

Each summer, I hike a short distance up and downriver, circling the cabin, trying to will a familiarity that, with time, will resemble the safety that everyone around me takes for granted. I carry pepper spray in my pocket. I rent a satellite phone. I check the bear safety books. I keep these tools, these charms against unreason, in a box near the stove. And if I only make it a few yards by myself before I return to the cabin, still I tell myself I am making progress. I am learning to live in a place I do not have to love, one that for the rest of my life, I can irrationally fear. For some passersby, the method and manner of my walking must certainly seem strange and incidental, even circuitous. But the vantage point changes with time. I see a little clearer in both directions, a distance that never quite moves with or against me. I watch it for all signs of calamity. Whatever responds to my changing scent, or the mud of my footprints, or the sound of my breathing, my voice in that place is strange and thin. Wherever I call from, it marks the place.

# Yes

I proposed to Cait and she said *Yes*. I walked along the Chicago River from the Michigan Avenue overpass, past the Loop, and down the rickety circular stairs under the balustrade, crossing stone planters glazed in slush and filled with cigarette butts, in Chicago's late December early dusk wondering already whether this was the best way to do it, the best place to spot her before she spotted me, some place I could sit and wait for her in the shadows, flowers in hand, a full smile and feeling dapper in my new wool slacks with the blue wool sweater I bought at the department store on my walk from the El because Chicago in December was colder than I remembered, the wind unforgiving and unimaginatively dull, my jacket and scarf and hat nothing against it, my cufflinks and watch nearly marble on my skin. And, *yes*, Cait was already making her way out of the museum and through the park,

along the path where my sister had ferried her. She was walking in one
direction at *Yes,* toward the place I knew, already, she would surely say
*Yes. Yes,* this must be the place. The benches were metal and bolted
into the pavement. The water was dark and lit on all sides by holiday
lights, a great pitch-black at the end of the channel where the harbor
became the Lake, hushing, at a distance, ice: *yes, yes, yes.* There was
music up on the avenue, someone singing loudly over a prerecorded
track. "God—*Yes! Thank you! God Bless!*—Ye Merry Gentlemen." No
boats out that hour patrolling the river to watch the tottering edge of
*Yes.* No sea monsters rising from the toxic and microbacterial sludge
of Lake Michigan to phosphorate a spectacular *Yes.* Would Cait find
the spot romantic? Would the stone wear through the fabric over
my knee as I bent down to look up? Would that one *Yes* become a
beautiful and definitive and lifelong *Yes*?

I stomped my feet and checked my watch. I dug my hands into my
pockets and rolled the ring box back and forth, losing it each time for
a quick second in the fumble of fingertips, grabbing onto the loose
thing to make sure it was still there before starting again in the other
direction. Cold hands, warm heart. Cold feet, bad shoes. Someone
was walking down the stairs: not Cait. A short man in a duster and
long scarf. He smiled at me. I thought, *He is dressed better than I
am.* We wished each other a happy new year. I turned and watched
him disappear up the next overpass, past the water and gone forever
from my life. Our life, *yes*? Had Chicago's skyline always looked so
lonely up close, the dark shrub of shorter, closer buildings near the
water, the old *Sun-Times* a wall of patchwork window lights, even
the Hancock rimmed in green and red windows for Christmas? And
what was the name now of the Sears Tower, blinking its ridiculous
antennae at planes and ships? Green: No. Red: Yes. I watched the
overpass for some sign of Cait. I checked the time on my phone. A
friend had said once that thousands of workers drowned to channel
the Chicago River. They floated up and swam to whoever stood in
the water, turning their faces toward the moon when the moon was

full of light. I listened for their song. I could hear the water, *Yes*, the cars and cabs passing on the avenue, *Yes*. My shoes scraping the black ice as I bounced on my heels. *Yes!*

*Yes*, of course Cait would say *Yes*. Hadn't I felt it before, the intoxicating certainty, the waiting and waiting and waiting for *Yes*, with all the unreason that made the feeling so vital? Could one *Yes* ever follow another *Yes*? What ended that ever definitively began with *Yes*? The certainty of feeling seemed the only feeling, so powerful I had to chase after it and reassure myself, over and over. *Yes. Yes*, we both wanted it. *Yes*, the spell. *Yes*, this easy leaning into each other in the cold air, huddling our warmth, holding out the ring she had picked weeks earlier with her cousin, the ring on her finger now, our strange urgency to get on with this smallest prelude to a life we meant to make together, this urgent and beautiful beginning of a life we were poised to claim in my midwestern city and take back west. *Yes*, and *Yes*, and *Yes*, I had arranged the whole visit. *Yes*, the best sort of question because I already knew the answer, *Yes*. I had only to say what I wanted and then ask for it. *Yes*. Cait was waiting to say *Yes*.

I had mumbled *Yes* to myself and family and friends and even the haircut guy. I had walked through my day, taking their confidence as divination itself, that the rest of the world waited to hear the news, full of approval, eager for *Yes*. I was positively beaming with *Yes*. I was radiating *Yes*. I felt it buzz my arms and chest. No, my pocket was buzzing with my sister's text message: "*Yes*, she's on her way." Cait was stepping out of the cab now, holding my hand-drawn map up to the light. She was turning down the stairs to find me. Here comes *Yes*. It can only be her, it can only be *Yes*. Even *Yes*, years later, I remember most clearly how, *Yes*, my chest burned as my heart beat nearly through it, the blood fast in my fingertips and ears, my whole body suddenly too hot under scarf, sweater, coat, and hat. I was having a stroke. No, I could see her, finally: *Yes*.

I tried to get down on one knee, but Cait pulled me upright. The wool on my leg scraped the bench and held together. She said we should sit together a while before we said anything after *Yes*, which we did, and we cried a little together, because it was so strange and unlike anything I had ever imagined a *Yes* would be. Were we celebrating now? I took out the box and put it on her lap. She opened the box, slid the ring onto her finger, and we leaned across each other like two old friends at a funeral, repeating our prayer: *yes, yes, yes, yes.* We called friends. We turned off our phones and watched the city. We walked back up the stairs, along the bridge, and into Chicago, even brighter up close, away from the moon and its impossible water, *Yes* and *Yes*, the perfect grid of streets and city lights that seemed to follow our spotlight across a stage, the perfect choreography, fast and slow, until there we were, *Yes*, together in my old city, walking quickly to keep warm on the other side of a life, done finally with our beginning, crossing from *Yes* to *Yes*.

# Signal and Noise

The Chicago doc's office closed a long hallway: two separate rooms combined decades earlier by taking down the wall between them. We talked every Friday by phone, though I only visited the office in person a dozen or so times. Even after he semiretired, moving into his home office a few blocks away, I still pictured him holding his phone on the worn sofa beside the books stacked on books, under his posters of Matisse, Van Gogh, various traveling exhibitions to the Art Institute, the famous statues that I recognized but that never came to mind except while I was waiting on the deeper sofa opposite him, ordering mentally the things I meant to talk about, trying to remember the names of his children and the places he went for vacation, while he finished making our tea. It was a nice touch, that tea. There was a silence in the room as we waited for the water to boil. Always, I stood in the hallway before a session deciding how I would start the conversation and what I should talk about next. Always, mug in hand, that anxiety slowed to a deep color of two or three important ideas, which came to seem less urgent than what I had imagined all week, as though so many years and chats now acted on the mind as a great distillery, concentrating the essences, wafting away other, lesser frustrations. The morning after I proposed to Cait, flush with well wishes, a different kind of distillation was already beginning. The Indiana nieces were reporting via text messages discord in Katie's family. With each rattling in my pocket and bright flash of the screen came the portent of still more calamity, reported as faint praise, surrounded on all sides by terrifying implications of guilt and widowhood.

"Why," the Chicago doc asked, "does it matter how anyone besides Cait or you feels about your decision to remarry?"

"It has to matter," I said. "For starters, I can't get any signal from all that noise."

We often started with this metaphor. Signal and noise. What were other people saying, and what did they really mean? What did I need to listen for and what could I ignore?

I said it was like listening to Wilco, *Revolver*, *Pet Sounds*. Drums and bass distorted through one speaker. Melodies and guitars cleanly out the other. Katie's family, hurt, and mine, well, thrilled. A third speaker: Cait's family, thrilled too. And every time I picked a speaker to listen to, I felt like I was betraying someone. I kept working the analogy, even as it fell apart. I knew the various solos by heart. I couldn't hear the whole song.

I shifted gears. I told the Chicago doc about my elaborate marriage proposal, Cait traveling from one Chicago landmark to the next, meeting my family and closest friends. How we took the early bus from Indiana, where my nieces had handed Cait the first clue and said their good-byes. It had mattered to me a great deal that they meet and like Cait before we got engaged; I wondered what

I would have done if they hadn't all so quickly taken to each other. Arriving in Chicago, Cait met Sheila at the bus station. They raced off together for coffee and carrot cake in Andersonville. Then Cait took the bus to meet Jeff at Wrigley Field. She walked with Dave and Meghan out to the park with the statues from the Wizard of Oz, where I had first called Cait to suggest our cross-country trip. All day, phone calls from friends in California clued Cait in to still another favorite spot or city standout, ending finally at the Art Institute lions, where my sister and her fiancé pointed Cait toward the balustrade. I had planned the day for months. I knew she would say yes. It was so corny and perfect. Even that morning, our phones had lit up with more good wishes and good cheer, the eager congratulations of people I didn't know, who admired my good taste and fortune.

"How," I asked the Chicago doc, "was the focus of this story my worry about Katie's family?"

That night, falling asleep, it had seemed possible that I might wake suddenly from a dream; that my life with Katie or in Indiana waited for me still on the other side of waking. And when I woke instead in Chicago, and saw the gray buildings through the window, the neon decorations down the block flickering off, I laid very still for a moment. What if Cait was not there? What if I had returned to Chicago without her? I wanted to remember the dream: something about California, happiness. And when I instead rolled across sleep and into Cait's body, I tried to enjoy all of it, to be happy and entirely of one life. I wanted that life to hold its shape long enough to seem certain, to sleep and wake and see the room again, find Cait and pull her close, and then doze for another hour or two, listening to the city begin its daily routines, filling with other lives continuing around this one.

What was I asking the Chicago doc to do if not to offer some strategy to keep the lives distinct?

The Chicago doc opened his eyes. How was he always so calm?

"So," he said, taking a sip of his tea, "what does it matter how anyone else besides you or Cait feels about your decision to remarry?"

\*

"The Marriagers," Cait's niece declared us. On our postcard wedding announcement, she pushed us in a shopping cart across a Costco parking lot. "We're Off the Market!" A few weeks later, we aimed scanners at price tags. We listed everyone we wanted to see at the wedding, and we invited all of them. In his chambers, over lunch, Cait's second cousin agreed to marry us. He was a widower too. I wanted to ask him whether there was something I should know about remarrying, as a widower, but he only offered advice to both of us. Spiritual counseling. Pastel worksheets to understand how we'd fight. At night, online, we picked colors for dresses. We ordered ties for groomsmen. I bought a new blazer. Cait picked a dress from the family stockpile of beautiful wedding dresses in the basement of her family home, some five or six decades old, from grandmothers, aunts, cousins, sisters. We drove as a family from the hotel where I made a toast with my groomsmen. Thanks to Katie. Blessings for the future.

In wedding photographs, the last of our youth hardens at the edges into modest early middle age. Handsome and confident, angular rather than round, we glow, beam, preen, lean. Our eager progression will never turn us back toward youth, but we feel young, so impossibly youthful and earnest and proud to love each other under the great apple tree, beside the aviary, and walking through the terraced gardens. Our wedding, the eleventh and last family wedding held in the backyard of Cait's family home, is a family affair. Five aunts, thirteen cousins, six siblings, ten nieces and nephews, and four parents do their part to make the day. Cait's mom plants new flowers everywhere and digs up the dying trees. She lays runners to decorate the fountain and to warn partygoers wandering the paths not to fall into the goldfish pond. All evening, our guests circle the gardens, under paper lanterns strung in the trees, between glass bulbs stuck high in the branches. My new brother-in-law climbs a stepladder to place the lanterns where they will shine out and over tables stacked with homemade cakes, candy, old china and silver platters, the bright salads dressed with wildflowers and herbs, shining up as the night comes on and fills the trees with their color. Cait's sister bakes nine cakes, the last, at my request, a Cubs cake. The other sister caters, with her friends, the dinner. "Welcome to the Borg," an uncle says the day before the wedding, as he climbs the stairs with a box of family photographs. Cait's grandfather, ninety-nine that August, is just awake from his afternoon nap. Before he rides his stationary bicycle, answers his daily mail, and heads down to the basement workshop to fix a chair, he wants to see the tie he wore to the last wedding.

*

We invited Katie's family to the wedding. We ate lunch together at the hotel. Cait's aunts sat with them at the rehearsal, and again during the wedding ceremony, as Katie's nieces played the welcome music and walked in the procession as flower girls. When Dave lit a candle and read a poem in Katie's memory, I tried to make eye contact with Katie's mom, but she was looking at her program. That evening, at the reception, a student walked up from campus and crashed the wedding. He was wearing soccer shorts and a Yankees hat. He insisted on taking a photo with the newlyweds. Until he walked off with a bottle of wine, I thought, *Surely, he belongs to someone at this wedding.* What harm had he really done?

Months later, the story of the crasher was an irreverent anecdote, a story we told about the wedding that said, "The more the merrier. We make a place for everyone." When I danced with Katie's mom, I smiled for our affection. She smiled back. I was so happy that she was there. But perhaps my happiness, up close, had some tint to it that did not resemble the old happiness. Or, there was an excitement to it that gleamed like ambition. Perhaps when she saw it, when all of Katie's family saw it, clearly and without hesitation, they felt separate of such happiness, foolish even. How patronizing: my brio, my gladly and loudly welcoming and wanting to include them. They did not want to only feel welcome. I married Cait and saw a bright, following future. They watched the wedding and they did not see the past. Or, they looked for the past and saw only my reverence for it, and felt bittersweet for such a mix of feelings. That we had danced together at Katie's wedding. That I had then known how to make their place at a wedding and now didn't.

That night, Katie's mom had hugged Cait's mom and said, "He doesn't need two mothers-in-law." While she did it, I danced in the garden with Ed and Katie's niece, though after a few more songs, we all left. Cait's sister drove us in the family Valiant to a nearby hotel, where friends had decorated the room with plastic and candy hearts. They had left two plates of cold dinner, which we ate in near silence, ravenous and exhausted, before sleeping a few hours. We woke early to catch our honeymoon flight.

∗

We found Lost Cities in a vintage gaming shop in the Sunset, on one of our city walkabouts. Lost Cities sold well, the owner explained, but it was not popular on the order of Life or Monopoly. Its niche was traditionalist gamers who knew and loved board games. The play was simple. Each color represented an expedition—white Himalaya, blue Antiquity, etc.—to remote or ancient places. The board held every expedition. There were two ways to play. The first was to simply beat the other person. Highest points won. The other way to play was to collaborate. Tacitly, each player might agree that his or her goals were mutual and exclusive. Playing to take away points made no sense. This version of the game was governed by luck of the draw. The difference in point totals was very small. Still, each player might score the near-maximum number of points. Like a basketball game played without defense, or a ballet consisting entirely of solos, there would be no tension, no adjusting and pushing back as the play continued. But wasn't that a nice way to work together, trusting the other person not to screw you and playing all the while for a personal best?

That strategy was no fun for me. I couldn't help competing. I wanted to look for mischief and misdirection. Was it a trap when Cait set out two or three handshakes of different colors? Did she hold points in those colors, or was she tricking me, distracting my attention from her endgame? After playing together all fall, I had developed the habits of a defensive and self-conscious investor, cutting my losses early, holding out irrational hope for some market weather that would revive my crops and turn everything, in the end, bright green. It rarely happened. I lost. Worse, I took losing personally. The cards were against me. My developments were unfairly stalled. Cait's straightforward play did not resist my scheming. Like water over a stone, she simply played across and through. I saw where the game might go, but so long as she did not overreach. There were no odds for me to bluff. I was playing against myself.

Day by day, we lost some of the evening light in the kitchen. We closed the windows as smaller throngs headed into the Mission or across the street to Dolores Park. A neighbor had planted a mock citrus down the block, and all the commotion seemed only to stir lemons and oranges across our room. On Wednesdays, our upstairs neighbors came downstairs to watch *Lost*. We made elaborate desserts to fete the last episodes. We enjoyed our truncated city life: high and pop culture, natural and urban spaces, organic meats and local produce, handmade jams with bread from the bakery across the street, and chocolates and ice creams at six or seven bucks a pop. Returning home, we took out Lost Cities. We opened the windows and listened to KFOG as the day wound down. We tallied the score, closed up the game, scrubbed down the kitchen, and set out everything to dry. Then, we climbed into bed, under our heavy comforter, with the cats on either side of us and the city below shining its lights up at the ceiling, as every few hours, an ambulance or fire truck ran across the emergency lane, which became at night, again, coincident with the sirens, the fastest way across our city.

*

On Katie's birthday, the second since her death, I had no clear sense of how to keep the day. I should invent my own rituals, the Chicago doc again suggested, and keep to them every year. But it didn't feel reverent to keep Katie's memory by myself. And what place exactly was I keeping for her in this newly remarried life? On her birthday and death anniversary, I wanted other people around me who had lost Katie too. But those people were in Indiana and Illinois. I had seen them a week earlier, for a fun run we hosted in Katie's hometown, and we had all gotten along fine. Here was the drawback to having fled everyone and everything for California. I was on my own. The year I had spent drawing Katie's family close to me, remembering her and spending some part of the day, week, month, birthday, and year in gentle commiseration became now my uncertain emotional homestead. Cait offered to take the whole day off to spend with me, but Cait and Katie had not been close friends, and I knew Cait would be worried for me, which would shift the emphasis. She hated to see me so sad.

After the fun run, I had gone with Ed, Katie's sister, and our nieces, to fly kites in a nearby park. It wasn't that Katie loved kites, but rather that we had all flown kites that first year on her birthday, at Katie's mom's house, outdoors but not too deep into nature. The point, I guess, was to get out ahead of the birthday, and so, for the day at least, grief. Ed pulled a couple of diamonds down out of the attic. We ran out the line and set the frames into their sleeves, before making tea and crossing the subdivision. The kites hung all afternoon in the sky, moving with the wind as we handed them back and forth. We agreed that we hadn't had so much luck with kites in a long while, and that evening, looking back on the day, it had felt like we had done well by Katie's memory: acknowledging the day, making it special, and then, letting it be.

In San Francisco, I went to the corner store and bought orange juice and Coca-Cola, two of Katie's favorites. I found the poem Katie liked and printed it on a small piece of cardstock. I woke early and stood a while at the chain-link fence of the urban garden behind my apartment building. The gardeners wouldn't come out for a couple of hours still. Row after near row was overgrown, abundant. From a field guide I had learned to name California Poppies, Purple Chinese Houses, Common Star Lilies, Blue Flaxes. I thought that if I stared long and hard enough, some miracle would arrive to endorse my spirit and confirm my good intentions so that anyone who didn't know me or Katie, which was everyone living in California, would see my earnest heart and mark my suffering and know the loss. Of course, that didn't happen. Still, I tipped both bottles through the metal webbing and said a quick prayer. I read the poem. I stood a while longer, and then I tossed the bottles into the recycling bins, walked up the hill, and ate breakfast by myself at a diner.

\*

On drives home from dinner with Cait's parents, or while walking back and forth across the city, we revised our timetables. We might try for a baby that winter. We should enjoy married life for at least a few weeks. Falling in love was fine and good, but we also meant to make a family, and the sooner we started, the bigger our family could be. One afternoon, Cait and I walked up to Coit Tower and watched a spaceman play his drum kit. Two boys pointed cameras and walked in circles. A diagonal walking path was cut into the hill behind him, and we could walk up it to one of the streets where the houses hid behind elegant gardens and empty driveways. The city was all steep hills and narrow corners, but at this high point, I could see everything. The bay sunk in fog. The coast stuck behind hills. It was the middle of the day and no one was home yet—no one would come home for a long while still—but I had the feeling of standing in a place to which the rest of the world gathered. I never wanted to leave that place. What was so great about a cold and rainy city on the edge of a peninsula that would one day fall into the ocean? Everyone who lived there knew. Anyone who visited knew. I felt like William Hurt asking Albert Brooks in *Broadcast News* what one does when the world exceeds his wildest dreams. "Keep it to yourself."

\*

Highway 280 was a steady shot down the peninsula between coastal hills and bay lands. We drove it at least once a week, for work and to see Cait's family. The later we headed back to San Francisco, the faster Cait fell asleep. At night, the cities between our cities rose to the exits in a cluster of lights, and then fell away beneath the underpasses. I was driving through that darkness and coming out, always, on the other side. I felt lucky and ashamed for liking my life in California so much.

I had the habit of getting overwhelmed and doing things I regretted, not magnificent violations of goodwill, but minor offenses I worried would accumulate into some kind of break with Cait, happiness, the city. Surely, I thought, it wasn't enough to have survived a tragedy and come out the other side. One day, I feared, I would be held to account. Something bad would follow something good. I couldn't think of another way to balance out the scale.

And yet, Cait was in the car next to me. She was dozing a little, but every few minutes she would wake up, smile at me, and nod off again. I put "Carolina on My Mind" on the stereo and let the song repeat. I thought about our trip across Montana and how I couldn't get sick of it. I let the memory of the trip settle in my mind and tried to figure out what would happen to us next. Time was linear. Already, it was running down a life. Sometimes, the Chicago doc would remind me that I had not orchestrated any of this, that I had neither anticipated nor invited the fact of Katie's death, but rather, I was living after it. In his explanation, it wasn't fortune I felt, but intense and crippling guilt, a feeling that assigned blame where there was none and made me both benefactor and accomplice to things in which I no longer played a part.

I refused to believe it. To not choose Cait—to believe she was merely some coincidence of timing and situation—meant accepting something awful about the nature of a world I believed now made us special. The truth was that I had no clue, really, what anyone was going to make of us. And if I had not yet quite figured out how to make my peace with that reality, then I also turned, whenever I could, to look at Cait. I let the feeling wash over me and I enjoyed the music, until we arrived outside the apartment, where I parked the car, opened the windows, and watched the city until she woke up.

*

*Noise. Signal.* I had always felt so superior to the rhetoric of therapy. I was a writer, and writers made their own explanations and contexts. So, it was humbling, week to week, to want so desperately to talk with the Chicago doc and to get so much meaning and help from him, worrying still there was some hokiness to therapy itself, a cookie-cutter philosophy that made the forms of suffering universal and Katie's death similar to other deaths. *It's all,* I sometimes snarked to myself, *a rich tapestry.* We didn't do word associations or trust falls or read *Iron John.* We did make connections everywhere and between everything. Doing so, I felt less alone. I wondered, the more we talked, whether what I wanted really was a benediction, some official permission to say, definitively, that Katie was *the past* and Cait was *the present,* or Katie's was the *first marriage* and Cait's was *the second marriage.* Were the words he used so different from the ones I hoped to discover on my own? I sat at my desk every morning to write. I read books he recommended: *Oresteia, The Noonday Demon, The Prophetic Imagination, The Rhetoric of Fiction.* I waited at that desk every Friday for his call. Sometimes, with his help, Katie came through as noise: in stories and the static of a continuing life. Other times, she was all signal: the fuzzy memory of a fight, a certain way she held her shoulders when she crossed a room, which I tried to fix in my mind, with his help, before she disappeared again. As soon as we got off the phone, signal and noise seemed to become two forms of forgetting. The signal was the memory. Time, passing, was the noise.

Sometimes while we talked, I looked at the books on my desk, the corkboard on the wall containing various maps and letters, Grandma's rosary, a strong poker hand fanned out catty corner from photographs I had pinned up and down one side of the frame. In a shot from our Peace Corps days, Cait and I stand in front of a temple. Her arm is wrapped around my waist. My palm is open and flat on her shoulder.

We are young and smiling, earnest and chaste, and there is plenty of space between our hips to see the road behind us, two men holding a map and talking to each other, a grove of trees, flowers. There is seemingly *no chemistry* in that photo. Still, I believed the story that I was learning to tell about us. We left the temple, South Asia, that life. We put the world between us. Our lives continued. And ten years later, when we crossed the country from opposite directions, arriving in rural Montana, we sought the beginning again, and not so eagerly and simply as we might have when we first met, and certainly no longer the picture of youth. We had only to start walking away from each other to draw the circle. We were already walking.

Some afternoons, I stopped into drugstores, found the deodorant aisle, and bought a new stick of Katie's favorite. *Baby powder.* I could only guess how so many pastes and heavy metals revived our long afternoon walks across the city, the essence of sweat under her collar, the coppery smell of her dark hair. They always did. What a rigged game to play, teasing certain memories while hoping not to find others, and knowing all the while that one day the trick wouldn't work. I would pull off the blue plastic cap and find only a sickly sweetness that smelled like nothing I remembered, and wonder that it had ever revived anything. How was it possible to remember the routines and habits of our life in such detail, but not the sound of her voice or the turn of her body? To see the potential for sorrow and loss in every precedent, and Katie forever her youthful and beautiful self; to live within such complexity and without sentiment, that such vulnerability might come to seem singular, and the rest of the world exceptional to it. What did it matter whether that was signal or noise?

\*

The day we decided to move into Cait's family home—where we married; where she was born; where her mother as a young girl had lived with four sisters, and lived still, taking care of Cait's grandfather—we walked a long loop through the neighborhoods near campus. We tested our new stroller, then sat on the front lawn with her parents, talking through the logistics of how everything might work. We were grateful for the help. We could live in the basement and share the kitchen. Afternoons, Cait's mom, Gail, said, it would be nice to sit with Cait's grandfather and talk a bit. He liked the company. We could make dinners together or eat on our own. We'd work it out.

Our room in the basement was airy and open, with new paint and carpeting, the original furnace, and stapled behind plywood, under ceiling pipes wrapped in white sheets, a panel of high-voltage wiring, by which a house built for no load so demanding as the single-coil toaster, 108 years later shuddered periodically to brownout, never quite failing its distribution to the televisions, computers, Internet routers, space heaters, minor appliances and major, semipermanent machinery of the brood that kept it. The house was warm and reliably accommodating, relied upon easily, and always ready to receive guests. There was space for us in the basement. Plenty of space. No one was prodigal here for too long.

It was not quite a custom to live in the basement, though most of Cait's cousins had done so, as had many of her uncles and aunts at the beginning of their own marriages. We were likely to live there at the end of the family's time in the house. Cait's grandfather, Sidney "Zait" Raffel, had paid cash for the house in 1955, a little less than ten thousand dollars. He had already once renewed its fifty-year lease on the land: two acres atop one of the campus's highest hills. Five days before Walt was born, Zait would celebrate his hundredth birthday. It would be his seventy-second year on the faculty. When he died, the family would have two years to sell the house and move out.

At night, the university did not turn on the streetlights so far from the campus quad, the better to discourage wandering students and insomniac athletes. The hill was a privilege, entirely remote from youth culture, which was how Cait remembered growing up there: among much older faculty members, listening to the parties a few blocks over on fraternity row. Most of the original neighbors were moved out now. The new neighbors were wealthier and younger, retired early to appointments and from startups whose shares they had recently cashed out for astronomical sums. The hill was a place for second, largely avocational careers. The magnificent gardens were tended by strangers: roses and palms; mighty elms, annuals and perennials. So much potential redundancy made Cait nervous. Our moving here could only be my idea. And it was. I wanted the help; to begin our life near *the Baby Whisperer*, as Gail was known to the legion of children and distant relations that came and went through her daycare in the living room of that Big House. The toys were still there, stacked in neat bins behind the television. Parents stopped in with their children, older now, to say hello. Sheepish teens still loved to dig out their old toys. We would do our best to fill in the deficit of youth and vigor once so predominate it overran an entire floor of the house.

Our first evening in the Big House, we ate dinner on the back porch. As a girl, Cait had gone bird-watching with her father. Over curry and rice, Bob now pointed to a tree, nearly as tall as the far hill, where two birds shared a nest. It had gone on like this for decades. The summer bird stripped the nest for the season, found its mate, raised its young, and hunted all season. Come winter, it flew south. The second bird built the abandoned nest thicker, kept its perch, and scanned the low brush for red berries and rodents. There was a place in the branches where the tree bent with the weight of the heavier nest, even in spring, but I could only make out, coming and going, the wide black wings of the summer bird, streaked along the back with crimson. I looked for what Roosevelt, arriving in the Badlands, had called *the cuneiform of wings*. I would look for it anytime I looked into the hills. The birds came and went. They made no clear patterns of their day, all the better to trick the interlopers, that a predator might learn to expect, among so much noise, so clear a signal. I was learning languages here: a family again, the start of my own family, a new family home. The bird built its nest high and away from the houses. A dark shadow was all it ever seemed to disappear into. With time, the shape of its progress came to seem obvious, even predictable. I watched the two birds for more than a difference of plumage, as though their sequence might surrender something of the season to my watching.

# The Big House

Last night your mother said, "Remember how much Walt liked the goldfish?" and I said, "So much," and she said, "Where did it go?" and I said, "The tape fell off the edges, so we took it down. Maybe look in the baby book," but we were both very tired from chasing you and your brother, and anyway, we haven't done the best job of keeping up the book since Sam came along, so probably the goldfish is gone, having served its purpose, though I remember the day we put it up so clearly. You were a little older than one. The picture was cut from an oversized wall calendar that your mother bought on clearance at the discount store. She had noticed how you liked animals, and we wanted to make a schedule of daycare handoffs, her classes, and my work. There was a big brown bear on the first page. She found online a picture of a dog and glued it in place so I wouldn't have to look at the bear all month. The next month came the goldfish you so loved:

bright orange on a white backdrop, in high relief and magnified to twenty times its size, entirely out of water and happy to draw your attention those mornings we would lay on the big bed considering it together, first thing, while your mother got dressed, you and I talking and tracing its imaginary path across the wall and out the door, into the garden where you liked to hose the plants and dig in your sandbox. Where would the goldfish go when he finally left? Could he make it all the way to the street, the golden hills, the coast, China? You didn't understand the questions. You pointed at the calendar. I said, "Goldfish." You smiled and kept pointing.

Your brother, Sam, is the same age now that you were then. How is he already so big and still so much smaller than I ever remember you? When you were this age, I flung you wildly in the air. I rolled around with you on the floor, and we went together to the burrito shop to eat giant plates of brown rice with black beans. At the bookstore, we looked at fire trucks and birds. We spent all day doing such mindless things together that the boredom seemed like it might kill me, and now you pace him for us, and he and I do the same things with a certain suggestion of nostalgia, and often you in tow. I suppose that's how it goes with younger siblings. We think he is a little younger than he actually is. Certainly, we take a little more care. Or, perhaps Sam is simply a different child: more sensitive and careful, less reckless. I think we are more relaxed when we parent our new one-year-old, though I might misremember that too. Already, another brother is on his way.

Just the other day, I got that wrong. I told a parent at your pre-school that you were only two years old. I confused your birthday with Sam's, which is earlier in the year, and then I worked the math in the wrong direction. I don't think that I confused it, really, more like a mistake floated a moment in my brain, dislodged from its school of likeminded wrong facts, and escaped quickly out of my mouth. How many times have I done that when talking about you? Switched two simple facts for each other, and not even realized my mistake until much later? More and more, I am afraid I will lose your entire childhood in such blunders of circumstance and time, or lose at least those twenty months that you were our first child, our only boy, our brand new baby with no hair, born so fast your round head came to us perfect and smooth. "Like a baby model," your aunt joked, "you could really make some money off of that kid." I thought, *No one can think his baby is so beautiful,* and instantly I knew I would have to work on my keen insights, my remarkable candor, because of course, everyone feels this way about his baby. And I get to feel it for you.

You were an early walker, yes, a gorgeous boy. The weekend we brought you home, Gail, your beloved Yu-Yu, went to the mountains for her two weeks at the family cabin, leaving us alone in the house with Linda and Zait as they rattled around upstairs, eating tinned fish and cake for dinner, watching *Walker, Texas Ranger.* You cried the whole night. We were so scared to be alone with you. We called the phone number on the hospital folder and talked with an advice nurse in Ohio. At three in the morning, she explained that probably you had some essential but treatable developmental delay in your digestive system. For the next year, we would have to spoon-feed you a powerful antacid in small doses, alternating formula and breast milk, and also, we should buy a probiotic to mix with the antifungal to promote the flora of something, and be sure not to give you too much of the antacid because, at adult strength, the medicine would fry your guts for sure, and then you'd *really* have a stomach problem. For the rest of your life, it would be hard, she said, but after a year or so, we could switch to organic whole milk and titrate the doses, trial and error like, until you either felt better or didn't. Or, the condition might resolve itself in a few days. Either way, we should definitely check in with our doctor after the weekend.

My god, we were terrified. You were up that whole night, sick, we thought, if not genuinely ill, though maybe you were just feeding off of our panic in that tiny basement room. I bounced you and bounced you until I lost my nerve—all that screaming, your red face—and when your mom took you and put you on the edge of the bed to rest a moment, rolling you back and forth, right off the edge you went, tumbling over the bedframe and onto the floor. We both looked at each other and thought, *This is it. We can't do it any worse.* The next morning, first thing, we loaded up the car and drove across California, into the mountains and up the hill to the family cabin by the lake, to find Yu-Yu, who met us at the car and carried you into the cabin. You went limp in her arms right away. She said she had never seen two adults look so exhausted, which we were, which is the sort of funny story one tells a child years later, knowing he won't really understand why we were so scared about something that worked out okay, which is, I think, more and more, the story of my own life. Of course, your stomach was fine. I wondered, even then, whether the nurse was messing with us, if hers wasn't a kind of black humor among those who answer the phones in Beaverdam, Ohio, at the witching hour, half asleep and abundant with caution, who chart worst-case scenarios against the dull repetitions of new parents and split the difference, searching the web for news and gossip as they nod and smile, laugh and wheedle and neutrally reassure. *It's fine. Go see the doctor. Go to the emergency room. Go back to sleep.*

"Does any of this ring a bell?" I asked you on a bike ride the other day. I wanted to know what you remembered of the Big House. You said, "Zaitie Candies," and I remembered right away something else I had forgotten: those giant bags of M&Ms we kept in the top drawer next to Zait's recliner, the one he would gingerly reach across with his homemade grabber (wooden plunger handle, nails, rubber bands, plastic claw) to pinch the edge of the bag and put a heaping scoop into your grubby paws as you smiled and jumped, climbing up onto his lap and prattling on about your day. There was a table next to the chair covered with all manner of balms and medicines. You knew not to touch them. Our first year in the Big House, Zait would come down the stairs still to ride his stationary bike, read mail, and watch television, sometimes even taking the Volvo down to the medical school to eat lunch with his old students, many of whom were also retired, a few dead: Zait the centenarian former dean in his derby cap and cane, and later, in his blue wheelchair, a red-and-black plaid university blanket across his lap to let everyone in the hospital know he was a big deal, ever dapper as back home, where he really held court, he took hours to get ready to receive his guests. Still, he always made time for you. He would pause to pull you up onto his lap, say a quick hello, and then gently call out to either of his daughters, "Come take the boy, won't you, dear? Down you go. Say dear, would you mind checking the mail?" and Linda would take your hand and lead you down the stairs to Gail or your mother or me, whoever was home from work at the time in our family commune, our multi-generation compound with the big guy upstairs in the Big House and us in the basement, sometimes just me and Sam playing in the living room that faced west, so bright in the afternoon that we had to close the curtains to keep from baking the sofas, where you would join our game but first send Sam upstairs to get his candies too.

"Zaitie Candies," you said you remembered, "and the birdies," because of course the Big House had an aviary. It was next to the trellis, along the wooded path by the cottage. "Welcome to Narnia," a friend used to joke every time he came over to visit. It is true that the yard was overgrown those last years, making rather a Hobbit home of coziness among the trees overhanging the stoop, the dense hedge of flowers and shrubs along the street, the persimmon and citrus trees down the side yard, where three tiers of garden sloped sharply to the road. There was oleander all up and down the drive, kumquats, a lemon tree struck by frost that produced sour, rindy fruit, and the magnificent Braeburn apple tree from which the family made all spring and summer every variety of crisp, pie, crumble, bake, and cake, the tree that died the summer we moved out and is now all stump. We would sneak under it and across the property to the neighbor's pool, a Busby Berkeley affair of slides and stones and trees and fountains, where you could wade in the shallow end while we all beat the heat. The neighbor convalesced in an empty room overlooking the pool. She would sometimes complain to the nurse, though Linda smoothed it over, as she always did. Linda was in cahoots with everyone at the Big House.

But I'm getting ahead of myself. I want to tell you a story about your beginnings in this world. I want to tell you that story now, before I forget any more of it, or before it simplifies into something that feels less important, a story that animates the past rather than reveals it, the three or four stories any parent thinks to tell if only to prove that he or she was there and paying attention: that you dressed like a fireman for two years straight, ate lentils with curry powder and raisins as often as meatballs and noodles and pie, that when you fell off the bed we drove you to the mountains and everything was just fine, because, like most new parents, we didn't know any better than to worry about things we hadn't yet figured out.

First, though, I want to tell you about your first home, that magnificent and ancient homestead, the Big House, in which you were the fourth and last generation of your mother's family to be born and to begin your childhood. I want you to know something about how we made our life there, and became a family, by ourselves and with everyone who lived in it: your mother and me and you and Sammy; Yu-Yu and Gunga, your grandparents; Gail's sister, Aunt Linda; and your great-grandfather, the mighty Zait, who until the day he died, 102 years old, rattled around the upstairs, reading medical journals and making his oil paintings to hang on the walls and along the staircases, writing complaints to doctors and utilities and consoling letters to the spouses of his dead students, more and more of whom he continued to outlive, until the evening he no longer did, that curious night we drove over from our new home with dinner for the family, only to find Gail sitting on the stairs, smiling at you and telling us that it was probably time. Later, when you asked where Zait had gone, she looked at you and said, "Belmont," the city where the nursing home had taken his body, which was a literal enough answer that you were satisfied with it. You never asked again.

This is not a story I want to embarrass or confuse you, or even worse, to bore you. There is so much love in this world for you. All the malevolence and unreason in the world doesn't hold a candle to such affection. And if I say "first life" and "second life," it is only to acknowledge a sequence. You were loved and beautiful right at the start of a life that now continues to begin, as any good creation story should, with mythos and wonder and fact, as beautiful and spontaneous as any theory of the universe that accounts for how nothing becomes something, transforming everything that wasn't into something that is, bending the light a little, spinning the planets, and slowly pulling the smallest things back into darkness, to disappear, as though they were never there to begin with.

The goldfish might see things differently. Surrounded by us, taking the measure of our routines when we noticed him, he survived all of the intervening months in his white square next to the calendar, until the calendar was no longer of use. I have my memory of what went well under his watch. All of the studies seem to agree that a child is shaped into whomever he will become by the age of two, and now that you are past that age, by that logic, the plaster is set and dried. Does it matter whether you remember that beautiful house, our time there, so long as you know that you were there, before you knew where *there* was? That now we are here? You may even wonder, *What was it like?*

You were born and raised in an idyll. You grew up in a beautiful home, surrounded by loving people who kept it well enough to see the idyll and compel your imagination. You lived there for three years: just long enough to see it with your own eyes. The first time I visited the Big House, I was floored by that place. Your mother and I weren't even dating. And even as I came to take it for granted—to see the Big House as ordinary and very typical in its own way, and exceptional in many other ways—I believed it *was* good for us, and very, very good for you. I *am* happy that you were born there. And here's the honest truth of the matter. What is there to do with any idyll besides love and then grow accustomed to it? I have to believe that's true. Otherwise, I'm not sure I'll ever understand why we chose to leave it before we had to.

\*

Your bed faced a door that opened into a magnificent garden, most of which you could not see through your window. We curtained the sill in the morning so that you'd sleep later, which you never did, and during the afternoons, when you also didn't. On the sill, in front of the curtain, was a painting of a rubber duck next to a framed photograph of your mother holding you in the hospital. The painting was a watercolor by your second cousin. In the photograph, I wedge beside you and your mama in the mechanical bed, smiling and leaning in, friendly, and surprisingly, seemingly at ease. What I remember of those first days is the certainty that I would drop or break you, that I might neglect you in some accidental yet entirely irrevocable way. I dashed around the maternity wing, asking every nurse I could corner to show me how she changed a diaper, or hushed a baby, or angled a bottle. I took notes and compared methods and tried to secret the complimentary pacifiers away, lest your jaw malform its ligature and leave you one day sucking dinners through straws. All those successive surgeries to help you smile. Such was my urgency, to find no comfort that most fathers worried in this way. My worry had to be exceptional. I came home that first night to sleep a few hours in the empty room in the basement, but raccoons had trashed the bathroom and tracked mud around the new crib. We had left the door open to circulate the late summer heat, as we did most nights, though the raccoons hadn't come before and they haven't returned since.

In the photo, I look tired and happy. Your mother, of course, is exhausted but she looks beautiful. You favor her, especially around the eyes. You have my nose and broad shoulders but most of you is your mother's, and I don't mind that. I rather like it. I trace so many good qualities of our family, as we raised you, to a lucky coincidence of resemblance and inheritance: that someone taught us, from the start, how to be a happy family for you so that, even if we didn't quite know it, we might study and watch the model, and mimic its moving pieces, learning the rest as we went at it, by suggestion or by force of habit.

Zait and his wife bought the Big House in 1955 so that it might become the family homestead. What it accumulated in the intervening sixty years was equal parts etymology and living museum. The Big House was big. It housed nearly everyone. I can't imagine how Zait saw what it would become any more than he saw the continuity of so many future years. And yet, they continued. On his hundredth birthday, family and friends gathered on the lawn to sing, eat, and drink together. That evening, he kept his routine, watching *Walker, Texas Ranger* and talking with his daughters about the relative virtues of slow-motion karate. "That Norris fellow," he liked to say, "is pretty good, don't you think?"

Those three years we lived in the Big House we got to know its every routine, habit, and peculiarity; in those immodest moments, sometimes my own, which accumulated every ideal to the flaws and perfections of intimate witness; in every way we knew and lived it, the Big House was a paradise, our founding myth, larger even than it looked: regal, antique. Even when the garden flooded, the foundation wore through, unrepaired, the roof leaked, and the water heater was shot, these were only the kind of problems that someone would have tried harder to solve if Zait hadn't been right at the end, or hadn't believed it for decades even when he wasn't, a sheer game of numbers he won, and won, and won. He refused to buy expensive hearing aids because he did not expect to get his money's worth out of wearing them. He canceled the insurance policy on the house and then reinstated it. Sometimes, I still forget how loudly we spoke to him; our voices, magnified, making a startling contrast in the normal speaking world. I remember the bright, even pitch of his voice, though, especially when he told stories and recited poems.

There is a low point of trees and overgrown shrubs just past your window where the water sometimes collected, with only the bright blue sky—it was nearly always sunny there—to frame it. In the converted garage out the other side of the basement, you poked around wrenches, nails, saws, acids. You hosed pots or looked under rocks for pill bugs in the garden behind the cottage where Gail and Bob lived. We called that cottage the Little House. Your mother was born there. When she was your age, she went back and forth for large family dinners in the Big House. As Gail kept the Big House going, she and Bob ate dinner with you and me and your brother and your mom and Zait and Linda, every night. After dinner, Gail or Linda sat up most nights with Zait late into the evening, watching television or reading, watching him I suppose but usually chatting and laughing with him—we could hear it through the ceiling. "Still breathing," Gail would sometimes joke in the morning, and if he was fully awake and beginning his long morning routine in the bathroom, she would disappear into the kitchen to soft boil an egg or plate his tinned fish with toast, and brew weak coffee. Always, Gail arranged his breakfast with the morning paper. She sat and waited for him, chatting on the phone with her sisters or reading a book, often watching you.

There was a grate in the hallway of the Big House that ran a vent to our apartment in the basement, the converted room and bath I cheerily referred to as our "garden apartment," though the family preferred its former moniker, "the Pain Cave." Pipes ran in both directions crosswise to the space. The ceiling over the television and sofa was wrapped in old white sheets. When I called my parents and siblings on Skype, I liked to joke that I was calling from the space station. My sister, your aunt, asked once, "So, how do you like your new family?" At such moments, I usually pivoted, reflexively, to you and your baby brother. "The boys," I would say, "love it here."

The lower garden flooded on the day of our wedding. That was the last time anyone tried to fill the goldfish pond. But the trees, in every direction, grew quite tall. From the living room, we could see all the way to the satellite dish that Zait's wife insisted the university paint light blue, the better for her afternoon view of the sky. Ami died the year I met your mother in the Peace Corps. Your mother smiles still when she tells me that Ami used to stuff food in the mouths of passing grandchildren, loved to spray prom dates with lawn hoses, and without fail stayed up every night in the living room playing solitaire until she won. A few weeks before our wedding, a little more than a year before you were born, your mother and I wound plastic flowers into the roof of the garden shack and painted it white. It is the character of the home into which you were born that anything could be made beautiful and used again.

*

From the living room, we heard coyotes at night. Sometimes I would see the campus ranger making a late patrol, shining a dash-mounted spotlight in slow loops to weed out any last student revelers. People died there, it was rumored, but you wouldn't know to look at the long hills filled with day hikers. There seemed so little vegetation to support wildlife, much less welcome it back. I used to walk you through those hills when you were a baby. The sun there was impossible in the morning. It shined down in every direction. No shade. You would sleep and fuss, however I adjusted the sun shade. I don't miss those walks, though I'm sure one day I will. What is amazing to me now is that we only saw mountain lions in silhouette on metal signs:

> *Fresh mountain lion tracks have been found in this area. You are advised to never hike alone. Keep children close to you. Do not approach, run from, cower, or place your hand near a mountain lion. Fight back if attacked.*

Up and down the hills we made the loop, saying hello to the other hikers, who smiled at you whenever I stopped to move the sun visor or dig out snacks. I never felt unsafe there, but I did sometimes pick up the pace when we walked alone. I suppose most hikers did.

When I was a boy, I liked safe spaces. I imagined a room in my heart—an actual room—into which I invited Jesus. We sat together. The room was red upholstery, velvet I think, all around. The windows were stained glass and simple. I sat in that room, radiating faith and love. What more could I want in the world? But I was not in the world. I was imagining a room that I never wanted to leave. Perhaps what I felt in that room was faith. It certainly wasn't religion. *In heaven,* I asked Jesus, *didn't time get boring? How did the dead keep track of time?* I never asked a teacher those questions. I didn't want to tell anyone how I imagined heaven, much less admit that I talked to Jesus about it. I suspected that my imagination was naïve or flawed or corrupt, a form of sinning unequal to the grace I felt in my safe space. "Scrupulosity," the Chicago doc calls it now. Then, "shame" felt much closer to the truth. Could such a room exist if I only imagined it? I prayed, suffered, desired, and denied, trying to divine an answer, but when I sat alone with Jesus, I felt, always, loved.

I loved our small room in the basement. I saw enough continuity in the Big House to suspect that there were answers to discover there too, that the Big House itself was one answer to that wellspring of questions from which my curiosity and terror arose. Not that the world was a place to fear or seek shelter from, but that my experience of the world was less vulnerable among people so loving and happy. It is an affection and happiness that I hope continues in our own family, and so, at the beginning of your life. I felt many things during the years we lived at the Big House, but unlike in my heart room, I never felt lonely there.

*

One afternoon, you fell off the hanging wheel on the playground near the Big House. You were so confident and strong on the sliding pole, which you called a "fire pole," of course. I was sure you'd do fine on the wheel. You were excited to try it. I lifted you up and let you hang on it a few seconds. You hung, laughing, until your fingers started to slip, and then I caught you. We did it again and again. The trick was that the wheel turned at an angle: you started on one side and swung around, down and up, back to the other. Each time, I helped to slow down your momentum just enough to let go and land back on the perch, more or less on your feet. The time you fell, I'm not sure whether the force of the turn threw you or if you just let go. Either way, you hit the dirt with quite a *thump*. It was one of those falls where the first thing I thought was, *oh shit*, and then my second reaction, for a split second, was to start to laugh. I checked you on the ground: legs, chest, arms, head, neck. Your neck was where everything hurt. Like a turtle, you just kept popping and wiggling your head. You were screaming, of course.

Even when you felt better and wanted to go back to the playground, I knew it wouldn't last. Your neck hurt to slide down the pole and touch the ladder, even just reaching for the bar. You would get a grip, sling your leg out, and stop mid-slide. You thought it was the fire pole that made your neck hurt, then the stairs, the slide, even the lower part of the climbing wall. Everything hurt. You waited for the pain to pass, inconsolable. You were so angry. There was no convincing you to quit. That night, falling asleep, you would roll over and wake yourself, grab your neck and yelp, and then just as quickly settle back and fall asleep.

In the end I took you to the doctor. A sprain. A simple diagnosis. Your neck hurt the next day, and for a while you were cautious on the wheel, but you kept going right back to it until you lost interest and moved on to the big slide and climbing wall. One evening I watched you take giant leaps into the surrounding sand, catching your legs under yourself and rolling forward, racing back up the ladder and out along the painted edge, the sand gathering in cupfuls at the toe of your sneakers, which trailed from the park to the car to the Big House. I carried you, limp and satisfied, inside and covered you for the night in your fire truck bedspread. It was both a terror and great comfort to me that you were always so physically willing to take risks, even after such an injury. I knew it meant that as you got older, you would be less likely to freeze at danger and more capable in the natural world. When your mother was your age, she would set out with her bigger cousins into the woods with a promise to come home at dinner. You'll do that too, one day, though for now you wing small notches in your belt, oblivious and confident, perfecting your form as each new leap throws sand across the previous divot, making the sand a little looser as you drop out of sight for a few seconds, lulling the confidence of a father who thinks, *He is fine. The next time I look over he will be standing again and racing back to the top.*

*

Rice at the burrito shop was either white or brown. I always ordered the white rice piled moderately high with black beans, fajita vegetables, diced tomatoes, corn relish, guacamole, and salad. It didn't look like so much food on the plate, but the staff took good care to stretch the burrito. You, too, never changed your order: brown rice, black beans. You refused to eat anything else. We did it every week, more or less, for our last two years in the Big House. Every Tuesday, after preschool, we split a large apple juice in two paper cups. If Raul was working the cash register, he comped the sides and asked you how you were doing. Sonja remembered your name too. I tried to remember to ask her about the teaching degree she'd start in the spring. Sonja comped us the apple juice too. Whoever was working the register, we usually paid a little less than ten dollars for our meal. When we changed preschools, we did it every Wednesday. Chipotle Wednesdays, you called it.

You liked the music they played over the loudspeakers. You liked to dance to certain songs when they came on, waving your arms back and forth, bobbing your head. It was not artful dancing, but we found a groove, in the booth, waist up, you trying to snap your fingers, both of us pumping our fists. I loved the way you smiled when you danced, rice on your chin. Your mom and I tried a few times to dance with you too: little dance parties in the bedroom or upstairs, while we made dinner. We used to do that all the time, just the two of us, in our apartment in the Mission in San Francisco. I loved that you loved to dance. You never drank much apple juice. When you were done eating and bored with dancing, you tried to climb on the stacked high chairs by the door, or if you were really tired, you would stand up from the booth, climb under the table, and run for the door. Magnetic locks. Double-latched. One time, you stood behind the giant water meters at the edge of the lot. I asked you what you were doing, and you said you were cooking beans and rice. You held out two scoops, and when I took them, you smiled. It was hell to ever get you back into the minivan. You were out cold before we left the parking lot.

Back at the Big House I would slip your shoes off your feet, unbuckle your seat belt, and scoop you into my arms, cradling your head into my shoulder. We would walk down the stairs, through the garden, and around to the side door, where I rolled you into the bed, covered your back, and tucked your plush monkey under your arm. Once, when your cousins accidentally took the monkey back to Berkeley, I drove north to the city and across the bay to get it back. It was the night the Giants won the World Series. Even in the fog, I could see the fireworks over AT&T Park, tiny bursts of brushed light that filled the sky and disappeared. Like in an old spy movie, I met the dad at the end of his driveway. I drove back through the city and down the peninsula, arriving home a few minutes before midnight. Everyone said I was crazy to have insisted on making the trip, but it is one of my favorite memories of your dopey and happy toddler face, how you reached out and grabbed the monkey, turned in the bed, and fell instantly asleep.

*

There was a stretch there, just after Sam was born, when you and I spent all day together, twelve or thirteen hours punctuated by a quick and quiet break in the afternoon. Often we would nap during that break, you in your Ikea toddler bed by the door, me in the king-sized bed across the room. I would settle you in bed with a bottle, after a few books. Usually, I could count on a half hour of rest. I had to be careful to be quiet enough that you would not hear me and so call out, or run around to my side of the bed. Still, I loved to see you, eye-level, staring up over the tall mattress. You would half-climb up to look me in the eye, or I would open my eyes and see your towhead and beautiful blue eyes, smiling. You were my 100 percent alarm clock. As I fell asleep, I would wake myself at least once to double-check the door was clicked shut, the lock turned, the blanket on your back. You couldn't turn the door handle yet, but you could wander into Zait's garage unchecked and grab all varieties of danger by the blade, beaker, or power cord. Always, you woke energized and loud, sometimes a little out of sorts. I woke charmed and lucky, always in a better mood; no better way to see the world again after sleep.

*

Why did we leave the Big House? There was no space for the new baby in the Pain Cave. We wanted our own place and had saved enough to rent one. We wanted to stake out on our own to find that first home that might one day become our own eventual big house, the next iteration of family dinners and kids' Christmas parties, a big garden with fruit trees and sandboxes and a terrace covered in planters, even our own fishpond. Instead, we moved into a condo two towns over. We put planters in the yard and moved all of our city furniture into the small rooms. We came back to the Big House every few days for dinners and afternoon hangouts. Toward the end, Gail installed baby monitors throughout the house, to keep tabs on Zait during the day. He had stopped coming downstairs. He worried that no one would hear him if he fell. We gave him a bell, then a small air horn, and finally, the monitors. The day he broke his ribs, I heard a kind of thumping, which I think was Zait signaling through the floors. I helped him into his chair, where he sat a while before we got him down the stairs and to the hospital. That was a year, I think, before he died. After that, Gail and Linda kept the monitors on day and night. Zait's daily routine—conversations, phone calls, naps—echoed throughout the house. He stayed mostly upstairs, shuffling between his bedroom and his office, dressing for the day and answering his mail, watching television at night and reading his journals, to whose editors he wrote elegant, if shorter, letters by longhand on his university stationary, at night watching *Walker, Texas Ranger* with his daughters, grandchildren, and great-grandchildren, who visited more frequently.

*

Your mother says we recognize instantly the people in our tribe. She means those lifelong friends we spend most of our lives seeking out. The tribe that she and I found together began in the Peace Corps and continues even today, as we find them, in all directions of an affection that means, as it did at our wedding, *the more the merrier.* Even her old roommate and I still go to movies every couple of months. No one really goes missing or is lost too long from that tribe. I found a part of it at the Big House. I married into it, and it is perhaps the most exotic quality of the family into which I married—the one that you and your brother now continue—that they are always in mind, somewhere in the world and loved, with kids and dogs and favorite beaches and playgrounds, in new cities and countries. Whoever is sick or well, arriving in or departing from the world, everyone is accounted for, even when they are gone and always remembered.

Katie and I never visited the Big House. We never met Gunga and Yu-Yu, Linda and Zaitie. Still, I like to think that Katie and I were a part of that tribe, in our own way, long before I loved your mother. We met up with her at Peace Corps reunions in Chicago and Wisconsin and once in Seattle, at a friend's wedding in a home with a family and character I recognize now as tribal too, with wild blackberries on the fence and a giant grill where we cooked whole salmon for the pre-wedding dinner, drinking whiskey on the back porch and sleeping in campers across the property. Katie used to say that she had made all the friends she needed by the age of nineteen. But then, at her funeral, a tribe, much larger than the one she described, arrived from around the world and then seemed to follow at a distance, clumped together in the procession, physical incarnations of each stage of her short life: childhood, school, work, whatever life continued past college. Separately, they did not seem any more a tribe than a clique, a minor cult whose purpose was fierce devotion to a loving memory, but it always surprised me how that tribe persisted; taken together they were every part of a life, and they kept her at the center.

Will you be mad at me one day because I loved someone before I loved your mother? Will you question my devotion to your mother and this life we have made for you? I wonder if there is any right way to talk with you about the fact that I was married before, and just as quickly I wonder, Will you really care? I think about what I don't know in the lives of my own family—what I might never know, but also, what I have sometimes imagined, those stories I tell myself when veracity and origin can never be substantiated. What is the right age at which to tell any of this to a child? Do I wait until you ask? Will I say the right things if you do? I imagine my default motive here is honesty, but also disclosure. I don't want you to feel that I have left anything out. That's one reason I want to tell you about the Big House now, before too much time passes and we live in other places, before the present moment becomes so large and inevitable that the *before* and *after* are less interesting to you. Like every part of parenting, I guess, I want to tell you what you need to know. I also don't want to say too much. Some things will only make sense when you're much older or when—if—they happen to you.

Perhaps, if you do read this, take what you need and discard the rest. Take into the world a history that makes the most sense to you and test it against everything else you know and learn, even me and my stories of this place that you might only remember for how we remember it. Remember yourself in it when we talk about you. Surely, I've done this with the sliver of a sliver of Zait's life that I witnessed during my time in the Big House. A whole life I do not know preceded our arrival there. A whole life you will know followed it. What else can a history do except work these few places where the sense seems most likely? And if you see, in the life before mine, and the marriage before this one, some sense of a precedent by which you might still make better or more sense, then I hope, please, that you'll go after it. I have made my record for you. It is surely imperfect. But it is honest. It is all that I know how to do. More than my desire for your happiness and well-being, your affection and need for the world, your companionship and friendship and care in it, I want you to know that I have been happy in my affection. There is an integrity to this life, however you need or want to inherit it, a life that you explain to yourself, as you take this life apart and strip it for yourself, so that it will seem beautiful and special and dear, as you are to me. Thank you for that. And if the rest of the story never quite makes sense, if you sort through what I know and find more questions than answers, then let me offer one last insistence.

Widowed—it is said—a happily married man remarries quickly. He loves marriage so well he rushes back to it, and seeks again merely the thing he knows. I don't think it's quite true. The mind might order things first and second, but the heart does not love in sequences. It seeks too many through lines. What I know about being a husband began with Katie and continued past that middle point between two marriages, about a year after her death, when I could not remain inconsolable. No single wire of grief stretched between the two marriages, making music as it moved. No dating profile near misses, faltering too-soons, or graveside speeches with flowers and rain neatly connected the end of one life to the beginning of the next. *Just think about the good parts,* I told myself at first, *and try not to let the rest go.* I wondered about the widower I was becoming, who knew so clearly the husband he meant to be next. I did not want to forget the husband I had been first and would never be again.

Your mother is mine. I love her dearly. I used to believe that I loved her more wisely and better after Katie's death, but that's the sort of thing a person needs to believe, or says when he is stuck a little between lives. I don't feel stuck. That first year in the Big House, I would sometimes sit at my desk and listen to music, think of Katie, and wait. When I grieved for her, the movements, so broad, were immediate and obvious. It felt honest and good to still feel grief and loneliness, guilt and horror. It made this life feel distant and fragile and remarkable. I feel more honest in any affection, even my love for you and your brothers, if I refuse the contradiction. I loved that life, and in my own way, I sometimes miss it. I suppose one day I may miss this life too, though never again will I miss anything in that same way. It is an old way, fit perfectly to another life, before this life began.

*

The door from your room into the garden was painted yellow. It stuck where the curtain rod chipped into the yellow wall. We opened it slowly to minimize the damage. You could squeeze your small body easily between the jam and edge, though you often took the long way through our room and up the stairs into the kitchen, out the kitchen door, and down the stone steps, under the laundry line and across the pavers. There was a small plastic sandbox whose lid made the shape of a frog. All green. His eyes were not painted. They were a good place to grab the cover and pull it open and shut, which you could just manage so gradually the eyes disappeared. Also, we forgot to cover it. So many animals and rainstorms dug into that sand. We waited for the end of spring to fill the box with fresh sand. It didn't rain for the five long months of summer on the peninsula, and when we kept the hose away and the sand covered, you and your brother had a long stretch to play daily in the yard of the Big House, whenever you liked it. The cement wall on the near side of the stairs up to the terrace made a good sunblock to the west. The high brick wall at the end of the foundation absorbed the rest of the sunlight. We dried our towels after swimming on the wire chairs and table, a set gift from my parents when we first moved in. Sometimes we sat there while you played in the sandbox.

Flowers and trees grew in the shade without much watering. Your mother could name all of them. You and I walked down to the lower garden to water from the hose with the low pressure, until you lost interest. If I put my thumb in the spigot you'd laugh. Years from now, you may still recognize some part of that garden as your native realm. I never bothered to learn the flora and fauna of my childhood home. I knew the flowers that spoke with my thumbs when I squeezed them gently, and the telltale shape of poison ivy. There is no poison ivy in

Northern California, but there is plenty of poison oak. The lawns are green with vast places for hiding. When we crossed between the houses, no one ever seemed home.

*

I make a witness of this first, very early part of your life so that you might imagine the things you will forget as this life continues. In a few hours, I'll pick you up from school, and we'll haggle over where we should go next and which songs to listen to and whether we should swing by Gail's place that night on our evening bike ride through the new neighborhood, which looks nothing like the old one, or head out again to the overpass and watch the cars racing below on the highway. It is so easy to love you, now. There is so much energy and unexpected grace in how you move through the world. Your mind is that great starting place: all sponge. Your most radical sense of the sequences around you begins and ends with love. Here, in your home after the Big House, there are impossible moments of compassion and oblivion that extend the tradition in present bloom: a garden, our tiny fish tank with two goldfish, this family, growing still in every direction. You are bright and small in that vast greenery. However aware, at whatever distance, you are already the very best of us. So perhaps you'll remember it all as a story. Here's how you might tell it.

The very old professor lived at the top of a hill in a big blue house with his eldest daughter, who never married, and his second eldest daughter, who was married and had four grown children. The hill faced east to the bay and west toward hills at the edge of the ocean. The professor was 102 years old on the day he died. He was blind in one eye but pretty sharp. He quoted Longfellow at dinners and lectured about microbiology in his sleep. Both daughters had traveled the world in their youth and returned as adults to live in their childhood home and care for their elderly father. The oldest daughter had many friends. She made driftwood horses and sold painted scarves to boutiques. Her sister had recently closed the daycare she ran in the Big House for more than twenty years. At various times in their lives, each of her children had moved back into the basement apartment, alone and with their families, in the years after the professor stopped renting the apartment to his students. Minor improvements—fresh paint, better wiring, new curtains and bath fixtures—successively made it almost a stand-alone residence, with a separate entrance and a closed door off the hallway up the stairs, but no kitchen, so everyone ate their meals together.

The house was the family home, always at holidays and birthdays, especially around meals. Dinner was served at 7:00 p.m. sharp, even after the professor had stopped coming down the stairs. Dinner contained a serving of fish or meat; fresh vegetables, but no eggplants or cucumbers; toast; and nothing too spicy. In practice, this meant crab cakes or flank steak, cooked potatoes, asparagus or broccoli or salad, white rolls, and a big dessert. When it was time for bed, your grandfather, the renowned herpetologist, sang you down the stairs to sleep. After the meal, if she was home, the eldest daughter would stay up late watching television and listening for the professor. He slept into the evening and used the intercom to call for her help. The rest of the time, the two sisters ran the house, managed their father's routines and finances, arranged his visitors and mail, moving meals up and down the stairs to his study when he was too weak to take the stairs, sitting up with him when he was sick. He lived well even at the end of his life. A little boy sometimes came up the stairs from the basement and sat with him and made everyone happy. The boy was happy.

# Unanswered Prayers

"Unanswered Prayers" was Katie's least favorite Garth Brooks song, the one that her friend's new husband, at the wedding, gave to the DJ in a pinch when he lost the first-dance CD. The husband was panicked and trying to do his best to play *anything* so that the dance might happen. Katie was the maid of honor. The song always reminded her of that moment, which became her memory of the wedding, and more than anything else, framed her understanding of the difficult marriage that followed. "Well," Katie would say, as she hung up the phone after talking with her friend about the latest crisis, "he did screw up their first dance song." Katie forgave strangers easily. She expected very little from them. But it was another thing entirely to disappoint the people she loved, as the husband had disappointed her friend. Katie held on to such disappointments. They marked a clear barrier between the people she loved and those she did not welcome into her life. For this reason, I think, Katie always tuned out "Unanswered Prayers" whenever it came on the radio. I sometimes listened to it by myself, driving back from campus in Miami or walking across Bucharest, on my way to and from work. I came to like it for its taboo place in our lives and also because I knew that we could never listen to it together.

Once, at a county fair in rural Washington, a Garth Brooks impersonator closed his set with "Unanswered Prayers." Katie and I were killing time before a different friend's wedding. As it always did, apparently, the audience sang along. Katie sang too. Perhaps hearing it live made it a different song to her. I had never before heard the song. I remember rolling my eyes at the lyrics, and puzzling a little that the song was such a fan favorite. "Unanswered Prayers" is Garth Brooks's paean to loving the one you're with, accepting the hand life deals you, and not sweating the small stuff. "Because," as Brooks explains at the end of every chorus, "some of God's greatest gifts are unanswered prayers."

Already, I feel a certain ironic contempt creeping into my consideration. I'm not sure I like it. "Unanswered Prayers" deals almost exclusively in clichés of sentiment. It is, by most measures, a pretty corny song. It is also beloved, widely. I used to feel like such a jerk when I mocked Katie's favorite country songs, but I also hated keeping my condemnations to myself. Then, it seemed less a matter of taste, and nearly an ethical issue, that any music be held to account and judged according to its worth. I was twenty-five. Everything seemed worthy of my judgment.

Country music is, by tradition, a rigid musical genre. Chord progressions rarely change. Lyrics follow a few common themes. Listeners expect a certain, conservative transparency: show us what we imagine are our best selves—modest, humble, short on cash, true to family, God, and country—and let us celebrate them together. We, who work hard all week, and drink hard all weekend, and pray hard on Sunday mornings, deserve such simplicity. Country music fans are intensely loyal. They know what they like. They buy a lot of records.

All of the country music that Cait enjoyed on our cross-country drive to California was new to her, a hodgepodge of my own favorites mixed with the songs that Katie liked to play sometimes in order to counter my snarkiness. To Cait, the songs were all awful, and for that particular awfulness, and perhaps also because we were falling in love while listening to them, the songs were wonderful. Cait felt no contempt for such obvious sentimentality. She enjoyed the ridiculous lyrics. Country music wasn't her thing, but then, what did it matter how we killed time on our road trip? Even as we took turns driving across Montana, Wyoming, Nevada, and eventually the Sierras, one of us sat in the passenger seat, toggling the playlist "Cait's country" on my iPod. We sang along to most of the choruses—"Whiskey for my men, beer for my horses!" and "Wheeeeh-White Lightning!"— which we knew pretty well after a few listens.

I did not play "Unanswered Prayers" on that cross-country trip. Even then, I wanted to keep something back. I don't quite remember when I started liking the song unironically, only that I listened to it far too often after Katie died. That certain distance I had learned to keep between loving things and pretending to love them seemed, in grief, a useless distinction, mere wasted energy that I had mis-devoted to preserving an idea of myself that no longer seemed true. After Katie's death, no one cared that I was the guy playing Garth Brooks and thinking about Katie. However the song remains one of the few remaining bridges between that life and this one, as perhaps only music can, "Unanswered Prayers" energized a whole range of emotional details in memory that I was eager to feel. Shame and guilt. Entitled and fragile and complicit. More than memories of ordinary days or recipes or even particular holidays, "Unanswered Prayers" persisted, vivid and particular, risking no contradictions.

\*

Why, then, is my affection for "Unanswered Prayers" such an emphatic secret? Partly, it is a matter of privacy. I am a little selfish, ungraciously holding back something that I want to remain only mine.

But the larger share of my hesitation comes down to a matter of taste. I am embarrassed, still, to like the song. I have a sense of what "Unanswered Prayers" means to me. Some nights, I worry that anyone will misunderstand that meaning. Other nights, I wish that I didn't enjoy the song's corny reassurances and pseudo-religious consolations. However I distinguish the practice of faith from the gnawing reluctances of secular adulthood, I hear still a pernicious, even cynical suggestion of piety in the lyrics. Who wouldn't choose what's best for himself? Why would God constantly second-guess certain intentions (high school girlfriends, prayers) but not others (cluster bombs, network television)? More to the point, I like good writing. "Unanswered Prayers," by that standard, falls pretty short. It misses rhymes and beats throughout. It abbreviates verses in the service of nailing down its wobbly hook. It stops and starts dramatically as it walks up and down the pentatonic scale, following Brooks's hokey vibrato. "Unanswered Prayers" looks falsely forward with the great hesitancies of schlock, before turning back to complacence as a form of virtue, which is to say it resists reticence and encourages blind nonthinking. Like most of Brooks hits, "Unanswered Prayers" works hard but, to appropriate the old retort, so do washing machines.

Worst of all, "Unanswered Prayers" makes of laziness, if not the absence of critical thought, then a near virtue. Its lyrics invite not only acquiescence to the sacred, the trusting of a divine will, but also suspicion at any feeling too closely articulated. One can almost hear, in the singing along, a collective relief at not working too hard to understand one's choices, the events to and from which a choice conspires, and any interconnected logic. Like the titular prayers, such effort is all mere grasping, bound to come up short. In the Brooksian worldview, life itself is essentially unknowable. The individual experience requires little articulation, except where it conforms to common experience. The complicated feeling, like the uncertain memory, is a poor approximation of larger, inevitable forces: chastity and family, humility, honors, and grace. In this way, "Unanswered Prayers" is nearly a fable. It brings into the fold anyone who willingly surrenders the particular and looks instead for the lesson. *Submit to God: something much larger and smarter than you is doing the heavy lifting.*

A few weeks before Sam's first birthday, I worked out the chord progression of "Unanswered Prayers" most of the way through the song. I sat with the guitar in my lap, staring earnestly at my toddler, singing to him sotto voce, subjecting his reptilian mind to rot. *These are unimaginative chord progressions,* I told myself, *matched to terrible lyrics making arguments you do not believe.* No doubt, I compelled my infant listener to be persuaded. Just as I rewarded his smiles with more attention, and held him when he cried, so I could not help singing my way through more than the first chorus without choking up. Listening to me sing as I tried to sing like Garth Brooks, Sam no doubt learned to associate joy with sorrow, and probably also to confuse them. In such moments, I made him complicit in my non-secret, at least until Cait entered the room to my crocodile tears and his bubbling smile, which maybe she mistook for simple affection crossed with a father's overwhelming pride. Isn't it what we both wanted to believe? In that moment, who was I to correct her?

# Not So Much

Last week, I dreamt that you needed the aerial off of our old Ford Focus. I wrote the whole dream out as soon as I woke up, but I couldn't remember enough of the details to make much sense. In the dream, it was winter but not cold. I felt a gnawing panic at seeing you, though I don't think I knew you were dead. We were standing in the parking lot outside of the Jewel-Osco in Chicago, near our old apartment, just long enough for me to jimmy the joint of the aerial and toss it to you. You were surprised at my handiness. You gave me a big hug, and when I held you, my fingers stretched all the way around your back. I woke suddenly, made my notes, and brewed my first cup of coffee. That afternoon, I crawled back into bed and took a nap, and when I woke again, I had forgotten all about the dream until I saw it written out in the notebook beside the bed.

*

I've been reading our old emails, trying to remember how we talked to each other. The sound of your voice comes first, full of promise, like the opening chords of a song on the radio I love but can't name just yet, and then your laugh, entirely yours, the music. Whoever told me that I would forget the sound of your voice first was wrong. I've never forgotten it. What I can no longer recall are the arrangements: how much taller I was than you when I stood next to you, how it felt to sit together on a sofa, who leaned into whom when we walked across a city. We did it often enough. I should remember. I thought the quality of memory would follow some magnitude of experience, that I might arrange the memories by frequency so that I would be least likely to forget those things we did the most often. Instead, it seems, memory falls away like a lost radio signal. The last parts, right up to your death, come through the clearest. Even now, when I make some explanation of my life with and after you, when I talk *around* you because I cannot stop myself from talking, it's your voice I hear first, and then your laugh, as though we are fixed in time to both, and the things you might say to me are still only what you could have said when you were alive.

You wouldn't care for this conversation I'm trying to start. For you, it would not be a conversation. You would sit and listen, nod and smile. You might ask me to be kind to your mother but not to dwell too much on the past. You would remind me to be careful of expecting too much from anyone and to remember my low tolerance and easy frustration. There would be a silence when you would not ask me to look after all those lives that accumulated around you, friends and colleagues and strangers on whom you made the most vivid impressions, who wrote me after your death to say such nice things. Those people you brought close because you listened so well, but also because you guarded, more than anything, against the obligations that came with needing other people. It was easy for you to give and be needed. With me, it's need first, and order. I wouldn't just pick up the phone and tell your friend, as you did, "No, you're not a bad parent. You're just having a hard time of it, like anyone." Or,

"It's okay to leave your husband for a little while. Go to the city and get your head straight." Everyone said you were a straight shooter, but I think that's more a reflection of how you made us feel—held to account—than what you said. You rarely told people what they did not want to hear.

If you speak at all when I imagine you, you say things like, "You could not have saved my life." I say, "Maybe." You smile at me in that way that means, *Well, we both know how this is going to end,* or you say it outright: "Really, John? A bear? You were going to stop a grizzly bear?" And we go back and forth like that, starting and stopping our fight, until that moment you decide to stop me dead in my tracks. "What does that night have to do with you *now,* John? *I'm* the one who died. *You* are the one who lived. I was killed by a fucking bear, and you married Cait and moved to California and started a big family, and you want anyone to say, still, 'Poor guy, he had a rough go of it, eh'?"

And I would want you also to say, "Isn't it enough, already, that year in Indiana and these eight years since? Can't you just fucking be happy—the boys, Cait, California, the writing and teaching—can't you get over yourself?" and if I could goad you into it, if I could make you snap, then I would know for sure that it's not really you talking. I would no longer recognize your voice. Of course, you never swore like that. You never lost your cool when you were really upset. What I would hear, instead, would be the sound of my voice as I have trained it to sound like yours and call back in those moments I run out my string, desperate for a signal.

\*

"You married the wrong Peace Corps Cait," you used to shrug at the end of a conversation, or as you crossed a room, or sometimes, as you leaned over to kiss me on the forehead, on your way up the stairs, turning back to say good night, when you enjoyed getting my goat, because you knew that I enjoyed letting it be gotten, and maybe, also, as a reminder that however well I enjoyed the joke, when some plan for the future came up—a family, a house, our hometowns—we were for now keeping at a distance those things we were not sure we wanted together. And I think our life would have continued like that, and we would have been happy in our own way, because when you died, I didn't think of the joke too often. It was only a year or so later that I began to think you knew me well enough to see several different paths to happiness and to lay them all out in front of me at the same time, to clue me in that however we fought, you wanted both my happiness, and also, whatever had made the fight worth having.

I know it is my own smallness of mind that seeks the reference point in meaning, that insists on comparing one marriage with the other in order to decide that one suits me better. Divorced men, apparently, do this quite often. Widows rarely remarry, but they too take the measure of a past, and often more acutely than widowers. At family events now we hardly talk about you. Someone asks about your family, whether I'm in touch with your mom or how your nieces are doing, but rarely do we talk too long about you, which I think is a kind of superstition against tragedy and loss. Not that we mean to avoid you, but since my life continues so well, we focus instead on the present.

"You married," Cait said the other night, "the most straightforward girl in the world," and it is one of our running jokes, that she is the even and calm one, and I'm the worrier. She is hopeful and I am filled with doubt. She sees the good in people who I worry are out to get me. She visits her mom, is adored by her students, and loves our boys and her husband, all of whom together make her feel happy and rooted and loved. I feel loved too, but I get prickly when I don't take time away from what I love, and eventually, from myself. I am a loner but she is an extrovert. Didn't you and I basically switch those roles when you were alive? You hated comparisons. You loved the world enough and felt secure enough in it. You did not need contrast in order to recognize the things you loved.

*

"Not so much," Beth wrote after you died, "is what we all remember you for saying. It was your kinder, gentler way of saying, 'No.' Katie, do you like syrup on your pancakes? 'Not so much.' Should we go out tonight to that club your friends like? 'Not so much.'" The night before you died, we went to the international movie theater and saw *Ocean's Thirteen*. We had dinner at the café with the pizzas and the tall beers. I opened my birthday presents a week early so that we wouldn't have to take them with us on our train ride into the mountains. We were at the beginning of a journey, just. That memory is where I go to find the conversations that might continue as something other than our last night together. I know what I want to ask you. I am thirty-nine years old now, remarried, a father. I live in California. I have written about you, and little else, for nine years.

"Are you happy," I might start, "for me?"

You would smile at the boys. You would let me ask other, self-congratulating questions.

"Could we have had any of this together, ever, us?"

But these would still be prelude—softballs. You would know it from my nervous eagerness to talk. You would sit across from me at the table, watching the lights turn on and off outside the movie theater, signaling us to come in, listening to the traffic, swirling the last sip of beer in your glass, waiting to hear me out, as I argue with myself, and when I am done delaying, you would smile at me—as *the painted ponies go up and down*—at how I argued with you every time you said one life had nothing to do with the next, that it could never just disappear, that it wasn't okay to sometimes find no meaning. Instead of singing more Joni Mitchell right back at me, you might see how it gets under my skin still. You know me well enough to wait a little longer. I cannot help myself. I have to ask it, if only to hurt you back. You listen for what I really came here to ask, because it means we still have something to talk about, if not quite say to each other. And whatever your answer, I would hear what I expect you to say, what I know you must say, even before I'm done with my question.

"Shouldn't I still wish you hadn't died?"

\*

When I meet new people, it is a long time, if ever, before they know about you. I like it this way. I hate explaining how you died, or worse, answering questions about the day, our last trip up the mountain, whether it was a black or brown bear. I can tell a reasonably straight-forward story about falling in love with Cait, which requires no detour through grief and violence. It is a sweet story. With time, it has become self-contained.

When you go missing in my stories, I notice your absence. It sometimes feels like a trick, to say so much about my life while leaving out one of the biggest parts. Doing so doesn't feel deceptive. I don't seize, racked with guilt. Part of what I mean to describe here is not grief at all, I think, but forgetting. The other day, while Cait made dessert, I said, "The year I lived in Bucharest..." and I was conscious right away that I had left you out, and probably Cait noticed it too, but so what? I knew she knew. I was talking about the coffee shop down the street from our apartment, the one we went to constantly, though in this particular memory, I went alone. I bought a kilogram of Easter candies, the most delicious milk candies I have ever tasted, and I walked into the park to eat them, listening to a radio interview with Paul McCartney, pausing at the intersection of the paths to admire the flower shops with tulips imported every few days from Turkey. Sometimes I brought them home for you because they were your favorites, but I don't think I did that day. I ate them all myself. I listened to Paul singing, "Kisses on the bottom..." and you worked late most of that Easter holiday. We went to that park at least once a week. You held my hand and leaned into my shoulder. Sometimes, you wore the blue windbreaker, the one your mother bought for you after Christmas, with the long zippers and shiny tags, but you always took it off and tied it around your waist after a few blocks because Bucharest never got that cold. What should I have said about you that afternoon that wouldn't consciously shift the conversation to your absence, that wouldn't feel like I had mentioned my past life only to mention you?

Ears prick at your name. Forks tap. Eyes dart to partners as games slow. It feels like stopping time itself to smile so resolutely and steady my voice, as words that once cast spells—*Katie, grief, bears, wife, absence*—now move like legislation between the head and heart, withstanding debates, inviting revisions and expansions almost as quickly as I can say them. Always, some incidental detail of the past forces a choice in the telling—*ours* or *mine, us* or *me, her* or *their* or *its*—that feels either too clever or discreet. Sometimes, I cannot find the connection to the present moment. Still, I speak as plainly as I can—nearly offhand. "You seem so friendly and happy," a colleague says one afternoon over lunch, "not like you've been through a big tragedy." I say it over and over again: "Yes, I am happy." Happier than I have any right to feel. And I never say the next thing that comes to mind, which seems in many ways just as true. I was happy before you died too.

Your name is a blessing. I say it now to mean a different life. Many people hear your name but not always the distinction. Or, they hear instead a harbinger. That life is short. We must enjoy what we can. Bad things are going to happen, and it is only a matter of time—hopefully a long time—until the person we love is going to die. Such sentiments are so obvious as to seem nearly clichés. They come from the other side of a consensus, however contemporary, about how and why death happens: that death is not exceptional, it is not experienced collectively, it does not shape a continuing life, the familiarity it invokes is neither healing nor reassuring. When I say your name, I do not mean to incant to the living. But I listen carefully to the questions that follow. Beyond what we tell each other, or say we mean and feel, the questions make a path between lives too. They let me know how much anyone really wants to know or understand.

\*

When the video rental shop in Chicago finally closed down, we bought ourselves a whole library of sad movies. They made a catalogue of, if not our best moments, then some of the least forgettable. *Moulin Rouge*, for the night you broke your toe trying to hurdle the leg of the sofa. *The English Patient*, after that terrible fight. *Waking the Dead*, for the night we walked out into Dhaka to find a city yet indifferent to our national tragedy and still willing to sell us bootleg DVDs. When I saw a good sad movie without you, I would call and tell you to meet me after work for the late show. Or, I would rent it and bring it home a few months later. Then, it would be a different season: Chicago, in full bloom, or Bucharest, gray and rainy, *The Eternal Sunshine of the Spotless Mind* missing something without all the snow. I was very good at guessing the movies you would like. You always picked the worst movies. The night you brought home *Hearts of Atlantis*, I was such a terrible snob. It wasn't a bad movie. I just felt superior. I guessed the ending, scene by scene, and you never let me forget it.

Can't I bring to mind some fantastic last memory, one that I can hold on to and say, after so much time, means we were happy and the end of your life was a good one? Even if life doesn't really work that way, can't I now at least be happy for us?

After a year in Indiana, I could not see still being the live-in uncle. My staying was sad and lonely. So was my leaving. And yet, what a beautiful last few days of *one last time* that summer became. Then, I was gone from Indiana. I was driving across America to California, and the short time I stayed in Missouri and South Dakota delayed only my sense that I should arrive at a beginning, far from any place I had ever been. California was new to me. The crossing itself was worth more than staying put. There were prospects out West: jobs, land, weather. Cait. My prospecting was linked with a past I made into an offering. I would never get free of it. I would not claim it. I would try to do better, if only that the end of one life—your life—might lead, finally, to the beginning, again, of mine.

The last memory that gets erased in *Eternal Sunshine of the Spotless Mind* is the moment that Joel and Clementine first meet, at a barbecue among mutual friends on the beaches of Montauk, New Jersey. Having spent the entire movie willing, then witnessing his memory being wiped clean in the reverse chronology of their relationship (revenge— she did the same), Joel arrives finally at the beginning. As the house around them falls apart, Clementine meta-reminds Joel that their knowing each other is about to be lost, and they agree to try to enjoy, rather than preserve, the moment of undoing. The sea rises to flood the living room. The roof is torn off. But even this good intention doesn't quite work out. Joel doubles back to the worry he felt the first time through. He apologizes, wishing he had acted differently. Clementine barrels forward, impressive and oblivious, to repeat the first mistake again, to start again the love they have, separately, in the waking world, already agreed to erase.

*

"Letting go," a friend says. "To hang on to B, we let go of A." I don't think it's quite true. I wanted you first. I chose you first. I wanted that marriage first, its affection and contrast first, and I loved you first, fully and without any sense of alternative, before I knew how to love anyone next. Then, I don't think I could have loved anyone better. And if I forget the rest—compress it into anecdote or hide it away in stories I tell too often, make my own cryptic shorthand, or sometimes simply refuse to tell—then such forgetting requires a good deal of imagination. I imagine the past in order to forget it. I fix the idea in my mind so long as it holds its shape without becoming eventually something else. I coax memory toward a reassuring plain of feeling and sense, where a life begins to move in an entirely different direction, and I mark the place where absence displaces a life. I will myself to find it again and again.

I pay Microsoft thirty dollars each year for the privilege of keeping our emails, dating back to the first year we met. In them, we never seem to duke it out or exhaust each other, go back over again and again our small and big fights as I do now, holding fast to our positions. All I ever find are short notes, usually sweet and generous. We remind each other of evening plans. We add to the grocery list and encourage each other about some work matter. We trade small jokes about some show we're going to watch or something a friend has done. It's possible that I destroyed the worst emails while you were still alive. I definitely didn't do it afterward. Perhaps, during our marriage, I shaped those letters to say what I wanted them to say about us and left out the rest. If that is true, then I was in some process of constant spin, an imagined presentation, or becoming, at which I strained to find myself by articulating who I imagined we were, and who I was beside you, because of it.

It is August. You would turn forty this year. I have a recurring dream. We are arriving to the end of a journey. It is San Francisco. The airport is only a minute or two away. We are happy. We take our bags and walk through an empty airport. No security. Antiseptic and modern walls, as though we are inside of some fantastic high-tech contraption no one yet knows we cannot live without. I am trying to say good-bye to everyone: my parents, my brother, my sister, their families, and finally, you. There is a spotlight on us. I can hardly see your face. I wake in my bedroom and the shade is up a little at the bottom of the window. I roll out of the light and pull the covers over my shoulder. The bed is warm, my place worn in. I must have hardly moved in the night. How could I want to be anywhere else? I turn in the bed toward Cait. I want to roll into her body and hold her. I want to sleep with her these few minutes before the boys wake and we draw straws for who will get up to make them breakfast, read books, put on a show. The room adjusts. It is clearer to me now. It is not morning, but late afternoon. I have fallen asleep reading on the bed. Cait has left the house to let me sleep. She has taken the boys to the park to meet our friends who are just back from a vacation. I can just remember the dream, enough to make it a story—the light and saying good-bye, the airport, white walls, my family, you—though I have no idea how much I have forgotten, those first or last parts of the dream that I cannot revive, more than the obvious departure. What does it matter how I sort out the rest? A few hours later, I can hardly remember the dream.

# The Lake

I am there, and Katie is not dead, and because it is late summer, we take turns jumping from the floating dock into the cold water, well clear of the buoys and the motorboats, in high season, kicking up their wake, buzz-sawing a light chop where the solstice's long shadows green the shallows clear to the lake bed and the balls of our feet scrape rocks as big as tortoise shells, scrape and bounce the silt but make no noise, and nothing lurks inside or below them because such nature is bountiful and welcoming, and seems to like that we are there. Behind us, trees, mostly firs and Jeffrey pines. Around the lake, the roofs of cabins and docks are stained to match their crowns. A larger lake borders this one, deeper at the far end, folding the sky around Katie as she shimmers the end of another shallow dive and comes up fast, smiling and laughing, a hint of mockery in that laugh, but always, mostly, joy. Often, when I dream of Katie, she is some place we knew together, an old apartment, a hike on the trail the day she died, but not this time. We race to the dock. The wood under my palms is smooth and warm as I pull up short, squinting into the bright sun at branches falling on the far side of the lake. A man is walking through the trees. He is swinging his chainsaw into the heavy limbs and stepping across their crowns. Power lines snap and pop beneath him. He is looking at me—at least, in my direction. The cup of the lake dips into the trees. The boats near the beach slow and tap. I know this place well enough to recognize it, and to know that my memory is out of place in the life that the dream contains. But my recognition is fast and loose. It loses shape as quickly as light on the lake changes color and jigsaws the reflections of trees, my face, Katie's bright and young face. Something near the man's chest—a badge? the edge of his saw?—catches the light and flashes, blinks and flashes again. I look away. The silence of his chainsaw is heartbreaking. I want the noise to start again, to hold together a few moments longer the edges of a world I know I am forgetting. I sink beneath the waterline. Where I try to surface, the dock over-shades the green sky.

*

The noise has stopped, as in my dream, and whatever continues past that silence changes pitch, ferrying a different life to a place I cannot return, not like that, probably never. I am here. It is four in the afternoon, fifty miles south of Paris, as far from the lake in my dream as I've ever traveled, and seven years to the day that Katie died. I am sleeping in a friend's house, trying to get well—head cold, pool water—and Cait has gone with our boys and host to the nearby gardens while I rest for our flight home the next morning. Fifteen hours, France to California, with a pregnant wife, an almost four-year-old, and his brother, just turned two. Someone should be sleeping. I was asleep.

Two men at work in the garden have stopped their machines and gone home for the day. They are rebuilding the wall between the house and the road where the center bricks have collapsed after an especially mild winter. From my window, I can see the pile of broken stones cut out from the corners and the road beyond it. Some new bricks are stacked to either side of the gap, alongside jackhammers, mechanical saws, an overturned wheelbarrow, and a mini-excavator the boys all morning have climbed up and down while pretending to dig out the yard and the front porch. They have never seen an excavator up close, they are thrilled and making noises, and soon enough, they are fighting over who gets to sit where and for how long a turn lasts. When our host asks if Cait would like to see the nearby gardens, the gardeners wave and smile their thanks. Cait promises the boys croissants and juice to make the walk. Walt eats a croissant with great reverence, from one end to the other, carefully unwrapping the darkest flakes, peeling away the center, while Sam eats croissants by the fistful, two and three at a time, dipping them in juice if we let him. We try not to let him. The boys race to the gate. Walt has blond hair and new glasses for our trip, with clunky plastic frames like mine. His body has stretched in the last two years from Sam's husky toddle to a lean boy's trim. Sam is strawberry blond, like me. He has his mother's beautiful blue eyes and a different kind of charisma than Walt, a better sense of strangers and how to charm them. Perhaps this is his lot in life, at least until his younger brother is born: to please everyone. When Cait kisses me and says good-bye, I can smell the sun in her hair. She is not so pregnant yet that it's hard to hug for very long without nearly toppling each other. I watch her turn the corner from the house, down the side lane, and into a field filled with lavender, irises, tulips, lupines.

Giverny is a dream at the end of our trip: no cars, no city, everywhere mostly nature, and then, a kind of nature I have only imagined while looking at postcards over my desk, next to photographs of Tangail and Bangkok and Bucharest and Delhi, a nature that travels well. I fold my shirt and pants, set the alarm on my phone, and shake two earplugs loose from a tub I have carried, in my suitcase, across Europe. The next morning, when we leave the house, I will remember the titles of books in the library, the bear-shaped pillow on each of the boys' beds, even the order of drawers and shelves where we stacked the dishes after dinner. But I will have no memory of the houses on the other side of the road.

Our bedroom is shaded and cool. The blanket and pillows are white with green trim. Every few minutes, a tiny French car barrels down the single-lane road and through the curve. However I stare at them, the drivers keep their eyes on the road. That the house has come into view through the gap in the wall is apparently old news. The road is narrow. There is little room to pass.

I fall asleep through the muffle of nearly avoided noises, and when I awaken, the silence that follows seems instantly to become the song of birds. *Songbirds*, I think to myself, *they are so beautiful*, though Cait later explains to Walt that the wrens and magpies of my imagination are ordinary pigeons nested in the rafters at the top of the house. They sleep there in summertime to be close to the cisterns. Their cooing makes a hierarchy among male birds hoping to scare each other off and isolate mates. *I am lucky to be here,* I tell myself, *the world has arranged my place here.* I chase a second dose of antibiotics with a tranquilizer, more or less following the hotel doctor's instructions. As the tranquilizer teases its first, pleasant fuzz, I move slowly, willing such pleasure to cling to the edges of everything, rise like a tide, and carry me past consciousness again, away from the continuing day.

*

How did we get to the lake in the dream? Katie would not have known the way. I must have taken her down the hill from Cait's family cabin, crossing the road, then the path from the beach, out to the docks that face the jumping rocks. In that dream world, Cait was surely our host, our dear friend from the Peace Corps who had invited us to California for a weekend of nostalgic remember-whens and then-and-nows. And if we headed back up the hill after dinner, we might have sat out on the porch with Cait, drinking whatever was left in the cupboards, at altitude feeling the liquor in minutes, passing a bag of chips to soak up the alcohol, taking our time to make a beautiful dinner. We would have asked Cait who she was dating, or perhaps her husband might be there too—her children, their friends, a whole separate life I know only in the dream, by coincidence and invitation.

Dinner at the cabin is lovely and slow. It comes together in stages, on the one or two burners that work, mixing whatever we bring with whatever we find in the pantry, in cookware schlepped up the hill from other kitchens and epochs each summer, alongside mattresses and dressers sent across on the rowboat. In the late 1980s, when the fridge went on the fritz, Cait's grandfather hired movers to bring a new model. With bungee cords and plywood they bound the white trunk to the center of the rowboat and swam alongside. The local newspaper ran a photograph the next week. The accompanying article is tacked to a beam on the door, next to a wall stickered with photographs of family and friends at various angles of repose on the decks, down at the lake, along most of the nearby trails into the mountains, and beyond that, the hundreds of square miles of federal wilderness with lakes named for islands, women, toys, birds.

There is a photo on that wall that I always spot first. In a sea of family, branching into one decade with an aunt, across the next and into the past with a great-cousin, Cait's lovely, young face turns easily past the camera. She is seventeen or eighteen, lounging with her siblings at a cocktail party, in a green evening gown with pearls. It is one in a series, from the same roll of film. Her mother and father are dressed to the nines. Someone is dancing out of focus, waist high. Her brother has more hair, and his cuffs are too long, but otherwise, everyone has aged well some twenty years later. My first visit to the cabin, I wondered, was this Cait's louche period? Her years of living dangerously? A storybook world of privilege seems to curl past the edges of the photo, a whole family history eager for discovery. "Oh," Cait said, "those were the braces years. I'm not smiling in any of the pictures." And then I saw the pattern, nearly a jigsaw across the wall, between vistas and shaggy outcrops, next to uncles holding trays of the day's cooked catch and nieces and nephews playing at the edge of the creek: Cait smiling, smiling, not smiling, smiling.

*

Would our dream's swim have earned a spot on the wall?

After dinner, Katie and I take sleeping bags onto the porch. The sky is bright. The air smells of smoke and dirt. The woods are lovely, dark, and deep again, and nothing encroaches them, or thinks to encroach our happy interloping: no bears, and also, no rockslides, thunderstorms, or wildfires in late season brightening the ridge. In the dream, unlike the waking life, I am not anxious there. I fear neither the cabin nor the woods nor the lake.

The back deck is clean and lined with sleeping bags on benches. Whoever arrives at any moment can swaddle into a good and easy place to sleep, a restful spot. Across the lake, a neighbor burns paper in the stove. He walks over the next morning to say hello and to discuss the water pressure: low this time of year, at the end of the snowmelt. Or, he invites us for dinner the next night. Sometimes, the neighbors at a different cabin will rally everyone to sit on their porch and play music. I can imagine that stretch of days and our place in it: pie at the Kennedys, drinks at the Botsfords, and a potluck at Sheila Nielsen's place. Sheila Nielsen, who owns the house in Giverny. She bought it a little less than a year after her husband, Chris, died. Fallen Leaf Lake borders Lake Tahoe to the south, near the state line, where Cait's grandfather bought a cabin on federal land in the early 1960s. She grew up hiking the Desolation Wilderness with cousins, packing family picnics to the beach, taking the rowboat across the smaller lake, and every few years, climbing the giant rocks to jump two, maybe three stories into deep glacial waters.

Every summer, Cait and I swim in the lake. We dig in the beach with our boys and hike to the natural spring or over the hill to drink lemonade at the store. At night, we sit by the stove, filling it with sticks and logs. We sleep under heavy blankets. And when there is bear scat on the trail, or if someone tells a story just back from a hike, I hole up in the car and drive to town. I wander the box stores for most of the day and get back early enough to see the path clearly around the lake and back to the cabin. But in the dream, I never think to fear the lake; the life I imagine is distinct from that fear and all of its distinctions. Absent a past I can think to remember, I enjoy the lake. And then, before I know it, I am awake again. The distinctions clarify instantly. I pull the comforter over my shoulders and wobble toward the window, where it's too soon yet for everyone to come back. Instead, I watch a world I do not recognize slowly sync with one I remember: silent machines, an overgrown garden, mighty and ambient scavenger birds. Beyond the wall, I can see what Sheila Nielsen explained that afternoon was the Seine, gray and flat against copper hills, filled at the far end with barges coming in and out of view. Words painted across shipping containers assemble into Cyrillic—or is it Turkish?—with the inverted consonants and doubled vowels, bobbing the waterline on red and blue and gray boxes that will be off-loaded, emptied, and filled again with whatever is missing on the other side of the world.

*

I spend that morning in an emergency room at the public hospital near Versailles. On a television in the corner of the waiting area, two talking heads make a detailed analysis of the World Cup. The Americans have blown a sure thing against Portugal, which either does or does not help France's chances to advance. The Americans have lost. That is the important thing.

In video highlights, a player tucks his nose into his jersey and shakes his head. Another player celebrates. The segment repeats on the quarter hour. I watch it nine times before a clerk at the receiving desk mispronounces my name and snaps a white wristband across my forearm. My name on the wristband is printed in reverse. My case is assigned the lowest priority of patient, a mere "bleu." The clerk points to a chart on the wall. Bleu means "wait." Red and yellow cases arrive at the hospital in ambulances and homemade splints, or carting oxygen tanks and talking on cheap flip phones, passing my place in the queue. I smile weakly and return to my seat. I want someone to understand that I am sick, and likely to get sicker, that it is a good thing I have been so proactive and arrived to the hospital first thing, at the first sign of symptoms, at the beginning of the infection. And yet, in such terms, the facts are plain and hard to make urgent. I am whining. I am stout and lucid, making my case. My ear will survive a day's wait. My meager bleu will not heat up and change color. I am no one's occasion for pity.

I wait for hours, watching the television, trying to calculate how many kilobytes of roaming data I lose each time I call Cait, check my email, or look online at the roster of the French national soccer team. Still more children from soccer matches, wheezing adults, and the obviously infirm arrive by ambulance with family members. They quickly disappear down one of the hallways. Their tags flash traffic lights on their wrists: red, yellow, red, red, yellow. Health service cards are laminated and printed on blue paper, with photographs in the top right corner. My wristband is paper and scrawled in cursive. It looks homemade, unofficial. Surely, they have no intention of actually treating me. They misspelled my name on purpose.

Back at the hotel, Cait chases the boys across our wing of the hotel, corralling their healthiest worst-case selves, post croissants and sausages, jam smeared, first to the pool, then into the television lounge, and finally, back to the free hotel breakfast. Where is her husband, the staff must surely whisper, that he leaves a pregnant woman to work like that? My god, he must be selfish. I feel stupid and self-important as I wait at the hospital. I check my status at the desk: still bleu. I have no more time in the day to be sick. We need to check out of the hotel, get our directions, and drive to Giverny. We need the boys to nap on the trip to prevent a total meltdown that evening. Who are these doctors to delay my getting well? Untreated, eager for a fight, I snap my wristband at the desk. It has no weight. It flits in the air like a maple seed and whirls across the floor, near the feet of a nurse who is talking to a doctor.

In the parking lot, I try to retrace my steps. I walk in circles, shaking my head at an angle, trying and failing to unclog the congestion. The clerk in the parking booth waves vaguely at a gate on the other side of the building. I cross a meditation garden with a walking path, large stones, hyacinths, French poppies swathing the grass in dark purples, oranges, greens, whites. I watch the rows of bumpers as I press the key, again and again, until finally a pair of headlights flash a dull yellow.

*

The night that Walt was born, it took exactly four minutes and eleven seconds to drive from the house to the hospital, the length of "Peace Train," start to finish. At that hour, there were no cars on the road. The radio DJ played one Cat Stevens song right into the next. To hear "Peace Train," one of Katie's favorite songs, on the way to the hospital, I told myself, was clearly a blessing. Katie was clearing the roads and the classic rock airwaves to wish us well. Our boy would be born that afternoon, maybe that night, no later than the next morning. The simplest line between two points was Cat Stevens.

In Receiving, a nurse took our driver's licenses and handed back two stickers with photos printed in the top right corner, black and white. I could enter this part of the hospital because I was listed on Cait's form. It wasn't enough, the nurse stressed, to be merely the father or the husband. The next night, through a translator, the patient who shared Cait's room kept telling a social worker that the form was wrong, things were fine, she wouldn't press charges, her husband sometimes lost his temper, but he could come any time he liked. We could see in the digital wash of the monitor two legs, two arms, a fist even, what might very well resemble a face. The nurse suggested we walk laps around the hospital and come back in a few hours. Or, the doctor would write a prescription for Cait to sleep a few hours, at home, until things really picked up. Either way, Cait was admitted now. They would hold her room.

We walked down one hallway, across the courtyard, past the emergency room, and into the basement. We counted stops for a toy train outside the pediatric oncology ward. Every time we entered a new wing, two security guards checked our stickers against their records on a laptop computer. The cafeteria was closed, but there was juice in the vending machines and large photos of student-athletes printed on neon blocks hanging on the far wall. "I knew him in high school," Cait said, nodding at a muscular boy in a tank top, "he was a really good swimmer but kind of a jerk." We backtracked to the entrance, turned down a different hallway, and found our way out a different exit. On one staircase, the sunrise split the hanging shades to make shadows on the floor. Where we crossed the shadows, our feet turned blue. Doctors and nurses changed shifts. A first wave of patients walked their ivs and rolled wheelchairs between the larger hospital and the smaller children's ward. We weaved between and through them, smiling at whoever made eye contact. Whenever Cait paused to lean against the hospital wall, closing her eyes and counting through her breaths, I put my hand on the small of her back and counted too. Back at the desk, we claimed our room. The nurse set the iv. An overtired anesthesiologist taped a needle to Cait's back to run the epidural. Cait felt better. She felt nothing. It wouldn't be too long now, another nurse said. We should try to get some rest.

I have never dreamt about Walt's birth. I remember it all perfectly, I think, especially the green and red fuzz stuck on our son's bald head, and the sock-puppet scrunch of his face at the middle, his eyes shining with antibacterial goop. An attending nurse stuck him under a heat lamp and covered his head in a blue-and-white cap. Our boy, our beautiful baby we liked so well that we rushed to have another one, and another quickly after that, seemed, at first, hardly real.

That night, while we were in the hospital, raccoons snuck through the side door of the house and ransacked the bathroom. I came home for a change of clothes and shower to discover muddy prints on the tile, muddy paper and towels in the sink, the cat hiding under bed, mewing hysterically. It took hours to bleach the bathroom and set everything back into place. I climbed into bed and slept through the afternoon. I knew I was awake because Cait had sent a photograph of our baby boy, just waking, wearing his cap. He was smiling, though of course, he couldn't smile yet, not really. My phone buzzed every few minutes on the nightstand. I could hardly hold my head up to look at it. "We become fathers all at once," a friend warned. "You don't really get ten months to prepare for it." I had a son. His name was Walt. The bathroom was clean. I took the Cat Stevens as my sign and climbed into bed, exhausted. The raccoon was a coincidence.

*

After we read the boys their bedtime stories, Sheila Nielsen makes us dessert, full-fat yogurt with dried cherries and bitter chocolate squares. We toss handfuls of the good stuff into the bowl and pour the yogurt over it. There is an espresso machine next to the sink and a drawer just below filled with different-colored cartridges. One color means triple strength, another decaffeinated, still another that the beans were harvested in a particular region of Kenya, organic and fair trade.

Sheila explains how, flush with insurance money at the start of a recession, she traced her lineage to a village south of Paris where her grandfather had practiced medicine and, on weekends, painted his neighbors by commission. The house was for sale at a discount, in need of work, and perhaps, the agent she contacted explained, a tad remote for an American vacationer. Within a few years, the house became a site of legend and pilgrimage for Sheila's friends. Word spread quickly of the roses in the cubby library cut fresh from the garden, the gardens down the street more or less unchanged from the famous paintings, the good books and framed photographs of rural France down every hallway, with men in bowler caps and women discussing the vote. "You will never live here," the house told its many visitors, "but what does that matter? You have visited. Stay as long as you'd like." In two rooms catty-corner to a long staircase, facing a portrait of a smirking woman wearing a white silk evening gown and heavy pearls, guests sleep under comforters, listening for crickets and the sigh of trees, and the ghost that Walt insists, right until he falls asleep, is waiting at the bottom of the staircase, next to the portrait, to eat us.

"Chris," Sheila says, "would never have let me buy this place. He worried too much about money."

The bowls are shallow and heavy. They rattle whenever we set them back on the stone countertop to make a fresh dish.

"A friend, he got sick at exactly the same time. His prognosis was grim. Chris was supposed to live longer, but Chris was always sick. His stomach thing—that probably didn't help."

That afternoon, Sheila offers me a blister packet of British pain medication, some mix of fever reducer and mild narcotic. Now, we are drinking wine. Cait asks a couple of times if I am feeling better, am I feeling okay, and I keep worrying, *Have I missed some important part of the conversation? Do I look especially unwell?* The thought of where I might possibly find emergency medical attention in rural France at the late hour becomes my nagging paranoia. I tell Cait that I am feeling great. I can't hear a thing out one side of my head and I am sweating like crazy with the fever, but I am not in pain. Only later do I realize that she is asking about the day: Katie. She worries about me while I listen to Sheila talk about Chris. For the moment, at least, I have forgotten all about the death anniversary.

"Now," Sheila says, "Chris is dead, and the friend is still in remission, which is good. I hear his charts look really good."

Before we head off to bed, Sheila tells the story of how she and Chris met. She was twenty and making her first trip to the lake with a boyfriend. Her boyfriend's family knew Chris's family. Chris invited everyone to the beach that afternoon. He was standing at the lake and passing out shovels, organizing a group dig to China. There were drinks, a barbecue. Someone made a fire. It went on for years like that, every summer, before he made his move, but that night, back at the cabin, Sheila decided she'd wait a few weeks and then break up with her boyfriend. Chris was magnificent: handsome, robust, charismatic, and so cheerful. The poor boy she was dating simply paled in comparison.

\*

Last year, it was vertigo. The year before that, bronchitis. The first year after Katie died, I woke in a fever with full nausea, hardly able to walk from the car to the nature preserve where we had spread Katie's ashes. I don't mean to get sick. A minor catch in my throat gums into place, however I hack and sniff. A ringing muffles to silence. There is a shooting pain down the right arm, or was it the left, near my back? Is that copper I taste? Am I bleeding? I know to be on guard for the month, right up to the day—that the day will approach with harbingers of illness and some minor but necessary treatment that passes quickly. When I left the nature preserve that first year, the fever was gone. The nausea cleared up that night. The next morning, I woke early and went for a run. A minor flu resolves itself in such a way. A twenty-four-hour bug runs its course. I know that these injuries, like a dream, are in some way self-conjured, but they are no less acute for their predictability, and I have no sense of their indication. That morning, in France, I pointed to my ear as the hospital nurse took my blood pressure. "Antibiotic. Airplane tomorrow." He shrugged. In broken English: "Medicine does not work this way."

Of course, it did. Or, I paid for it to work that way. The ear was bright red. The hotel doctor said the throat looked bad too. So, I had my diagnosis, my gift: my bauble with a bauble hidden inside of it and more baubles to swallow three times a day, for seven days, with food or a glass of milk. I was sick! I would get better! A quick stop at the chemist, and we were off to Giverny, following directions from a dashboard computer that took us along the most scenic route. Who was I still to be a widower that afternoon when my life continued so beautifully through sunflower fields and small towns with hand-painted signs? When I loved it so much, and felt, for all my easy susceptibility to viruses and infections, the buildup of a different antibody, one that perhaps accumulated also to something beyond a fever pitch, if just as impermanent? What was that gap in time I burned across, and across which I refused to look, that I felt in my bones such eager forgetting?

*

In the dream, Katie is standing on the beach. She is wrapping her hair in a towel and leaning over to shake the water out of her ear, with that little half shake I can't quite mimic. She pulls a chair out from under the trees and sits in the sun, half watching me, nodding off. Katie could sleep anywhere.

"Why are you doing this?" she asks. I sit down next to her. "Why can't you take your happy life and leave me alone already?"

"I don't know," I say.

"You do," she says. "There's nothing wrong with you."

"I'm sick."

"You were sick. For a while. Sort of. You're not sick now."

"I was *sick*."

"But you were never *really* sick. Not sick-sick. Just, you know, sick enough to worry a little."

The scar on Katie's forehead, that little half-moon she dug out that time with her brother—how could I have forgotten it?

"But the marriage itself, our life—"

"John," she says, interrupting me as she folds her towel over her shoes and walks toward the water. "You do this every year."

"A widower should not feel this way," I say, "about his dead wife."

"You like marriage," she says, swimming toward the dock. "Everyone knew you'd get married again."

"A widower should not feel this way about his dead wife."

"I know," she says. She is laughing, a little out of breath. "You already said that."

*

After supper, we wash the wine glasses and coffee mugs by hand. We load the dishes and pack the chicken into plastic tubs with the last of the salad. We will leave in the morning first thing. Outside, where there is no light from a city, the twilight deepens. The sky positively glows. Beneath it, a broken wall, a road, the houses and the river and the freighters, the hills and mountains, the beaches further to the ocean, all of it shades to a single darkness. The longest evening of the year finally begins. This is the exact moment when Katie died, and in another hour or so, when that moment passes, I will feel again a relief greater than I feel any right to expect. The weight will lift for a while, and with it, my reverent and neurotic attention to it, and all of the ways that Katie's death makes me feel terrified, lonely, uncertain, and worst of all, special.

We are returning tomorrow to the world: California, our home. The first day of another year since Katie died will begin with the simplest forms of persuasion and distraction, those that should only work on small children. Katie's death will seem again at a distance. I may not dream of her for months.

The boys will sleep in the room next to us. When they awaken, as they usually do, Cait and I will fumble through the darkness to the table with pacifiers and juice cups and sugary medicines, in the narrow sliver of the night-light, and do our best to offer them some proper consolation. We will sit with them and rub their backs, telling them stories or singing them songs until they fall back asleep. And if there is no noise when we walk into their room, if they have fallen back to sleep mid-cry, or soothed themselves enough to forget the distraction without our help, then all the better that we leave in silence. They will wake with the first light or just before it, and our day will continue.

I know what the light was that made the noise in my dream stop. It is clear to me now. A piece of metal sparks on the machine. The gleam of a mirror wobbles across my blanket. The Seine shakes out its still and deep waters, west of here, as the white sky over France grows bright with the first of the day's light in California. The light traps its cities in the heat, making the brimming white radiance grow broader and broader until all dissolves in it, all vanishes, all passes and either disappears forever or becomes something else. I should still be standing on the dock, shaking with cold, searching the water for something I have missed. Sleep, that brief stretch of blank hours that consciousness does not track, that grateful silence broken by light, makes its own edge with the day and draws two worlds across it, cleaves them with sharp teeth and makes them fall into darkness.

At the bright edge of memory, both sides fall together and away. Between them is a narrowing no wider than the space between the door and the floor. The door swings easily. It makes no noise. Our boys can come into the room to find us. I know Cait is sleeping next to me. The real world I imagine returns like memory to fill in the gap. The garden grows in patches of green and white, dirt and shade, field and flower, the whole way around the house, across the gap, wherever it finds the light.

# Mountain Rain

Our third son is born on a Wednesday morning, Cait's shortest labor yet. There is some bleeding afterward, and a surgery, but Cait comes through, exhausted and more than a little tired of boys, of pregnancy, of a body that loses and finds again its shape, so perhaps this too is an ending—a family of five, no more babies?—or perhaps it is merely another beginning, the start of our family life in full and earnest, a time I think at best can last a decade before our tiny men race toward their adult lives, across the country and world to places I hope we'll visit, where we'll wish them well and from which I'll hope at least for letters, news, sweethearts: a continuity, the continuing of a life we've started, as it finds several new beginnings. Like the other boys, Monty sleeps next to the bed, in a co-sleeper I've again adjusted to match the height of our mattress. The co-sleeper is held in place with two long straps across the box spring, the better for Cait to half-wake and nurse before setting him down another few hours. Under our overcautious watch, it took Walt forever to settle, so we've left Sam and Monty to fuss and work it out, and they are better sleepers for it. Before morning, footfalls, bowls of cereal, and shows, before the routine sets us off to preschool and teaching and long weeks on little sleep that pass in the blink of an eye, even those short days we get the boys early from Gail and take a picnic for lunch, or drive out to the bay lands to feed the ducks and name the Star Wars characters, imagining among tankers and bridges a perfect Lego spaceship burning across the sky, disappearing into a tiny moon of light, Cait and I get a few minutes together every couple of mornings. We thrill at such waking. We wake disoriented and confused—where are our boys? we have children, right?—and only after we tick through the shortlist do we relish such silence.

*

I give a talk at Cait's school. The theme is "spread the word," and someone has heard me speak elsewhere about grief and guilt, fear and hope. Before an auditorium of tenth and eleventh grade English classes, I start with Aeschylus—"It is against our wills that we become wise"—and continue with poetry, William Henry Wright, John Lennon, the Peace Corps, the beginnings of lives that begin again and again. Even the therapist in Indiana with the turquoise jewelry makes an appearance. I add in photos of stuffed animals, Horcruxes, Cait, koans, and grief. As always, I apologize for mentioning the two things I know that my audience already knows. Katie is dead. She was killed by a bear. I memorize the whole thing and deliver it in twenty minutes. All of my eight years fit into a single talk I practice until it sounds unrehearsed. It is the Chicago doc who suggests Aeschylus. I refer to him in the talk as "a wise friend."

Mom calls and asks again when I will write the happy book, the one about the wife and kids after the incomprehensible loss, and California, with the happy ending and all the silence of beautiful things happening outside of a need to chronicle, analyze, and share them with anyone. I want to say that I'm writing that book—*I'm always trying to write that book, Mom*—but what I say instead is that that book may never exist. I may never write that book. So, we change the subject and talk about Walt's glasses, Sam's vocabulary, Monty's smile and short naps, and how excited we are to see her and Dad when they come to visit in a few weeks. As we say good-bye, I ask her for a cookie recipe that I remember from childhood. A few weeks later, she sends a box of them, freshly baked, with a book about dragons for the boys and some candy hearts and a card for Valentine's Day. The boys shake the card in front of Monty's face. They coo and practice their baby talk, and sometimes, at night, they get wild and scrap with each other, bellow and wail and caterwaul, and the Chicago doc says it's probably because Cait is spending so much time with the baby and we're all getting back to work, and a behaviorist reminds us we cannot change our children, we can only change their environment, routines, and schedules, but in the end, their punches look pulled and they end up building Star Wars ships out of Legos and demanding more juice. We buy a pop-up trampoline. We build a reading nook in the corner of the room. A week later, we move the sofa into the garage and sit together at the kitchen table, holding hands and talking about our days.

At night, when the boys can't sleep, I prop my phone in a cup on the bookshelf and play a seventeen-minute nature sounds loop. "Mountain Rain." It's as much white noise as any mountain or rain I've ever witnessed, and it never stops restarting. I've played it 1,257 times, over and over again, a blank static that fills the space between their two beds with the facsimile of a natural world that still terrifies me. All this time I've spent entering it, under Cait's watch, in a part of the world absent those terrors that kept me from it, that beautiful world I cannot bear to remember, and still I am afraid. I imagine sometimes that when Walt is older, after his brothers have left the house too, I will walk into the woods by myself and spend days there, relieved of the obligation to protect anyone besides myself. There, I will know what it means to be vulnerable and selfish together, in a way that risks no danger for my boys. Perhaps Cait will wait for me there so that the end of my long walk will be my arrival to her, a fantastic story we will tell the boys later about a place I feel finally I have earned the right to live with and past, a place that is entirely my own, where they can come as grown men, able and sure of the woods, which is to say, like their mother at the very beginning: expert and wise, ready to care for me and make me feel safe.

*

Every couple of weeks, I take down Katie's chess set and line the pieces in front of Walt. We tick in sequence through their strengths and weaknesses. Walt likes the queen the best. He can't stop counting the spaces on the board. When we move our pieces, I am careful to correct the sloughing diagonals of the bishops, the meandering rooks, the ridiculous el of the knights, which we call horses, as my father taught me. I move my son's hand again and again in simple shapes that elude him. The process is maddening—such simple mistakes. I want to correct it. I want him to learn the right way to play. He is five years old. Every time Sam slams a taken pawn onto the kitchen table, announcing that he has destroyed yet another stormtrooper, Walt corrects him. Not *stormtroopers. Horses.* He marches his pawns down the lane and asks for a second queen, a third, fifth, and tenth. We switch out buttons, salt and pepper shakers, Lego men with lightsabers and silly hats who move freely in every direction and capture a move at a time every other piece. Left to his own devices, Walt would trade out all of the pawns for knickknacks.

Shouldn't he believe this about the world, that nothing in a life is ever lost, it only changes into something better, or is turned in a different direction, as the people we love, in turn, are loved by someone else?

When I put the board back up on the bookcase, I tidy the pieces of my shrine. It has not changed in years. I don't think my son even sees the shrine, only the place where the chessboard is stored: high on a shelf, just out of reach. If one day he reaches for it, or if he is curious at all about what else he sees there, I will try to make some sense of the

life it marks. For now, we only look together inside the box. We play
along its top. We use its pieces, and when we are finished, I assemble
the shrine again. I follow my son out of the room.

*

Hiking back down the trail from the lake, Cait and I make plans for
the coming year. Walt will start kindergarten. Sam will go full-time
to preschool. Gail will watch Monty, but probably we should arrange
some daycare too. Cait will ask Nadia if there is space. She liked Walt
and Sam, so perhaps it will work. And what about a regular babysit-
ter? Couldn't we offer to keep one on a kind of retainer, four hours
every Friday whether she comes or not? Cait will teach every day.
I will teach my schedule and try still to write. A woman in a black
swimsuit is stopped on the path in front of us. She is talking quietly
to her friend, who is standing off the trail, up the hill. "Down by the
trash cans," she says, nodding to us. "The cub is just behind it." Seven
years we have come to this place and finally it is happening. I grab
two giant stones from the trail, and we all stop to watch. "Is it a black
bear or a brown bear?" I ask. I know the answer. "A black bear," the
woman says, a brown-faced black bear. "They must have come up from
the dumpsters. I called out to the Turner cabin, but there's no one
there." It would be foolish to throw my rocks and attract the bear's
attention. I can do nothing in this moment except watch, and after
we watch a while, Cait and I start walking again down the trail. Our
cabin is maybe four hundred yards away, up the hill and across the
river. I clench the rocks in both hands and walk into the cabin holding
them at my side. I walk back out to the car and drive into town, and
when I get there, I turn around and drive back to the cabin. Who will
keep my family safe? The adrenaline makes me nuts. I can't sit still,
and Cait knows better than to say anything to anyone about it. So
we don't. Or, I don't. I disappear into the bedroom, take a pill, and
watch a baseball documentary on my laptop. The woman in the black
swimsuit kept watching, long after we walked away. I weep hysterically
when the documentary is happy and again when it is sad. What is

the difference? And when I feel nothing, I hear again her voice, and feel ashamed that there is nothing to say or to tell anyone that they do not already know or will believe, even if I say it, and in this way I keep my secret from everyone else in the cabin, because I am blessed and fortunate to live, and to feel alive, and to come here every summer and feel exempt from the things that I know surround us. Bears, but also a way of living, a pattern of days circling lakes and trails around which whole cities develop, from which the bears retreat until we are so numerous they must return, scavenge our waste, and become still another possible side of fortune, that we see them whether or not they mean to reveal themselves to us, that they suggest a different kind of abundance, an overwhelming beauty indistinguishable from terror. "Ahh," the woman said, whispering to us, "isn't it cute?"

*

Already, Monty has slept the longest in the co-sleeper. We'd move him into the boys' room except Cait is worried about all the pillows Sam likes to lay on the baby's face—to make his bed soft, to love him more than he needs to or can stand to be loved—and the noise of three small boys in one room. The potential for chaos, and barring that, mere calamity, stuns us into another quiet night. He'll leave our family bed soon enough. A few more weeks, a month maybe, and we'll pop the crib up again down the hall. We'll close the door at night and greet him with bright, cheerful sounds in the morning, and he'll learn to sleep through the night and expect us as the room brightens, right after the first light. He'll learn to call for us.

For now, he locks onto me first thing. He is smiling—all smiles. He leans and lists, slumps and drools, and the smile looks like it will never stop crossing his gorgeous face. I want that moment of total attention, simple and undivided, to last forever. Of course, it can't. Already, I am crossing the room. The bigger boys are turning over juice cups and smashing the wall with brooms. Cait is sitting at the table to nurse Monty before she leaves for work, when I will take him over to Gail's apartment down the street and head off to work myself. Always, after they watch their morning shows, the boys are restless. Monty is hungry. I can only look to the future a few moments at a time; when I am lucky, a whole afternoon. The world is changing too fast ever to really begin or end, but when I try to slow it down enough to hold the moment in my affection, always, it seems, I am looking at the next beginning.

To order or obtain more information on these or other University of Nebraska Press titles, visit nebraskapress.unl.edu.

CPSIA information can be obtained
at www.ICGtesting.com
Printed in the USA
FSOW01n1601201216
28755FS